BORDERLANDS

First published in 1998

Gracewing
Fowler Wright Books
2 Southern Avenue, Leominster,
Herefordshire, HR6 0QF

ISBN 0 85244 475 3

Designed and typeset by The Visual Works,
Ludlow.

Printed by Cromwell Press, Trowbridge,
Wiltshire, BA14 0XB.

GRACE GUIDES
ON BRITISH HERITAGE

BORDERLANDS

**The History
and Romance
of the
Herefordshire
Marches**

GABRIEL ALINGTON
Illustrations by
DOMINIC HARBOUR

Ludlow

Wigmore

Lingen

Kington

Leominster

Bromyard

Bredwardine

Stanford Bishop

Dorstone

Hereford

Peterchurch

R.Dore

R.Lugg

R.Frome

Abbey Dore

R.Wye

Llanthony

Grosmont

Skenfrith

White Castle

Goodrich

R.Teme

CONTENTS

Arthur's Stone

THE NEW STONE AGE, THE NEOLITHIC AGE, was an age of invasion, of colonisation, of migrant tribes from Europe and Asia heading for Britain in search of land. They came in small numbers, tribal families washed ashore in their rough canoes having braved strange seas for an island they can only have hoped was there.

The earliest known invaders were Iberian in origin, small, dark people who came from southern Europe. At first they settled in the south of the country, probably on the more open ground where the soil was light enough to cultivate with their primitive mattocks and antler picks. But gradually, through the centuries, they spread north and west to the Borderlands. Few relics from that age have come to light - a small collection of stone implements at Ledbury, a stone hammer at Kington, an assortment of arrow heads at Vowchurch and Oldcastle - but there are a number of Neolithic tombs.

The Iberians believed in reincarnation, that the spirit would return to live again, and they buried their dead in underground tunnels to await rebirth. These burial mounds, which are sometimes referred to as barrows or tumps, were built of huge boulders lined up side by side to form the walls with a 'cromlech', a sheltering stone, across the top. The whole construction was covered with a thick layer of earth so that the tump looked like a small rounded hill. The later Bronze Age burial mounds were generally longer than those dating from the Neolithic Age. There are several examples of Bronze Age mounds on the Long Mynd in Shropshire.

The finest Neolithic burial mound in the Borderlands is Arthur's Tomb. It was built about five thousand years ago, high on a ridge above the village of Dorstone in west Herefordshire. Through time the surrounding earth has fallen away so that the huge limestone boulders stand above the ground. The size of them is astonishing; most of all the cromlech, the toplid, which now has broken in two, but was once a single slab 6 metres long; its estimated weight is 25 tons.

Somehow, by commitment, by will-power, by working as a team, or perhaps by a combination of all three, the small Iberians managed to drag each giant boulder, possibly for miles, and heave it into place.

The Border Forts

THERE ARE SAID TO BE MORE hill forts and castles in the Borderlands than in any other part of England. And, though in many cases the hill forts have merged into the countryside and few of the castles have survived, it may well be true. For the history of the region, since its distant past, has been of conflict; the threat of invasion from hostile tribes, from foreign armies, of local feuding, large scale wars. Besides the shape of the landscape, the long ranges of rolling hills that rim the river valleys like shallow bowls, offer a wealth of vantage points.

The earliest of the forts belong to the Iron Age, the period from roughly 600 BC to the Roman invasion in 43 A.D., when tribes of Celts were migrating to Britain from central Europe. The Celts were great fighters, strong, fearless and bloodthirsty, they used weapons of iron, decapitating their victims with their mighty swords. Their tribal armies swept through the country, northwards and westwards, seizing and occupying land, driving the earlier settlers, those they spared, into Wales and Ireland.

There were a number of different Celtic tribes, the most powerful being the Brythons, who arrived in the latter part of the Iron Age and who generally dominated the other Celts. Which probably explains why, eventually, the whole country became known as Britain.

Unlike their predecessors, the Neolithic Iberians, who dug burial chambers, and then the Bronze Age 'Beaker' people, named for their buried drinking cups, who set up the great stone circles such as Avebury and Stonehenge, the warlike Celts concentrated their energies on building forts.

These were, in fact, not buildings at all. The Celts did not go in for stonework strongholds, they used the terrain. They created forts from hills, building them up in a series of ramparts one above another, each rampart ringed by a ditch. Some lower-lying forts had only one rampart; these are termed univallate. Those with two are bivallate, with three or more, multivallate. At intervals around the outer ramparts are entrances leading into the fort; these were inturned, formed to curve inwards for added protection,

The early settlers, the small, dark Iberians, who fled from the Celts and took refuge in the Welsh and Irish hills, became the 'little people' of Celtic legend, the dark fairies, sinister and will-o'-the-wisp, who, unseen, snatched babies from their cradles and stole pails of milk.

(Later, in the second half of the fifth century, when those Celtic Britons who had escaped from the Saxon invaders, fled to northern France, they gave both their name and their Celtic language to Brittany.)

particularly against the sling warfare practised at that time. A well-aimed sling shot could strike with terrible and deadly force. A good example of inturned entrances can be found at Ivington, three miles south of Leominster. There the large, multivallate fort follows the contours of the south-west end of the ridge. And, with persistence and a bit of luck, you will see that, as well as through the outer ramparts on the north-east side, the entrance through the inner rampart is also inturned.

Where possible the Celts built their forts above a scarp, a high, steep slope, unassailable to the enemy. Croft Ambrey at Aymestrey, has a high scarp on its western side; the Iron Age fort at Eaton Bishop crowns a steep-sided promontory on the south bank of the Wye. A site that overlooked a river was another advantage. Rivers, the Wye and the Lugg in particular, were the main routes through the densely wooded land. Sutton Walls, the univallate fort close to the church at Sutton Saint Nicholas, has a view right across the flood plain of the Lugg.

Some hill forts cover a huge area. At Colwall the Hereford Beacon, a multivallate fort which is part of the Malvern Hills, encloses 32 acres of land. Here an odd feature is that the surrounding ditch is on the inside rather than, as usual, on the outside. Another fort almost as large is Little Doward Camp at Ganarew in south Herefordshire, an area of 26 acres. But this is one where the original outline is hard to find for, as long ago as the 19th century, footpaths were cut through the ramparts and at the same time the original fortification on the north-west side was replaced by a straight upright bank. Not far from Hereford city and less than a mile south-west of Aconbury church, is Aconbury Camp, a single-rampart fort of over 17 acres. Here too the outline is obscure for the mound is thickly wooded, but with determination, if you push through the tangled undergrowth, the entrances on the southern side can still be found.

From the relics discovered inside the majority of hill forts, it seems that not only soldiers lived within the ramparts. Tribal families joined the fighting men, protected and basically self-contained, growing their own crops, grazing their stock, making pottery, spinning and weaving cloth. At Sutton Walls bone weaving-combs, spindlewhorls and loom weights made of clay have come to light, pointing to a whole weaving industry there. At Eastnor, where the bivallate fort spreads across the summit of both Midsummer and Hollybush Hills, excavations have produced shards of Iron Age pottery. And wandering over this fort, here and there you notice dips in the ground. These, it is believed, were the sites of Celtic dwellings, beehive-shaped huts, thatched with branches, basic homes.

Somehow it is details like this that bring the hill forts to life, that make it easier to catch the atmosphere. One's ability to conjure up the past varies, of course, from fort to fort, with the weather, with one's mood. But possibly the site which seems most readily charged with atmosphere is Croft Ambrey.

Choose a clear day, or one with broken cloud when the cloud shadows slide across the land. Walk up through School Wood along the lane - the area belongs to the National Trust - and branch off to the left following the path between the trees. Climb the stile and soon, beyond the wood, you reach the west side of the fort. Below you is the scarp dropping sharply to the valley far below. Before you go on towards Croft Castle on the east side of the fort, stop and look westwards at the view. Look out across the fields, the village of Aymestrey, the scattered farms, to the lines of hills. They curve round the skyline, north and south, range after range, rising, dipping, fading into the distance, into Wales.

That's the way they'll come, the hostile tribes, the enemy. Watch the far woods. Can you spot movement, the glint of metal, catch faint sounds carried on the wind? And behind you, footsteps, - someone approaching, more and more footsteps, hurrying, thudding on the ground, the clink of armour, voices shouting, loud, growing louder, closer, closer...

For a moment the past is very real.

Offa's Dyke

IN THE DARK AGES, the time between the Roman occupation and the Norman invasion, England was divided into seven kingdoms, autonomous kingdoms each with their own government and king. The Borderlands were part of Mercia, the most powerful kingdom, a vast area stretching from East Anglia across to Wales. The Welsh, mainly Celts driven out by the Saxon tribes who swept westwards across most of the region in the fifth century, were generally hostile, constantly attacking across the border, devastating property, stealing stock. To counter this and to define his border, Offa the 8th century king of Mercia, organised the building of a dyke, an earthbank nearly 238 kilometres long that stretched from Prestatyn in north Wales right down to Sedbury on the river Severn in Gloucestershire.

It was a huge operation, the construction of the dyke. It was designed as a continuous structure but, because of its length and the fact that it took between ten and twelve years to complete, the different teams working on it were not always coordinated. There are wide variations in the height of the bank, which in places was as much as eight metres. Some sections even had a stone wall along the top. And the ditch, which was about two metres deep, was sometimes on the inside and sometimes on the outside of the bank. There are also gaps where the dyke does not exist, probably where the woodland was then so dense it acted as a natural barrier.

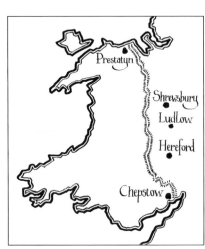

During his reign, from 757 to 796, Offa did a great deal to strengthen the power of Mercia. Generally early historians considered him a good king; he was a Christian, strong, civilised, enlightened. Alcuin, the 8th century English scholar, told of his interest in education and his encouragement of learning. He also had dealings with Charlemagne, the King of the Franks and the first western emperor. A letter from Charlemagne to Offa asking for a further consignment of woollen cloaks of the same size - a hint that there should be no stinting on the

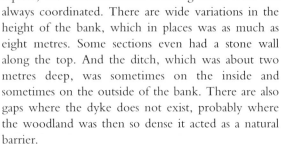

Prestatyn

Shrewsbury

Ludlow

Hereford

Chepstow

amount of cloth? - shows that trade was already established between the two kingdoms. In return Charlemagne promised to send 'black stones', which were probably large flat stones from the river Rhine suitable for grinding corn.

But a dark shadow hangs over Offa's life. He committed murder, a planned, cold-blooded and deliberate killing, and the victim was another Christian king, the young king of East Anglia, Ethelbert.

In 794, when Ethelbert was fourteen, he travelled to Mercia to ask for the hand of Offa's daughter, Alfthrytha, in marriage. When he arrived at Offa's headquarters, believed to have been at Sutton Walls, he was welcomed by a member of the court named Winbertus. Having come in peace, Ethelbert willingly agreed to disarm before being taken to see the King. At once the doors were locked behind him, he was bound and beaten. And beheaded with his own sword.

Afterwards, according to early medieval chronicles, Offa was overcome with remorse.

And to underline Offa's wretchedness, soon after the murder, came reports of miracles; a column of light seen shining over the marsh where Ethelbert's body had been dumped, the sudden restoration of sight to a blind man who, wandering into the marsh, had stumbled on Ethelbert's severed head and picked it up.

But it seems that Offa was not the only one responsible for Ethelbert's death. The Benedictine monk, Florence of Worcester, writing in the 12th century, told of Offa's queen, Cynefritha, urging her husband to believe that Ethelbert had come with evil intent, with designs on Mercia, to add it to his own kingdom of East Anglia. And Offa, who was politically ambitious and concerned at any risk to his authority, had agreed that the murder should be carried out.

Afterwards Offa had his queen thrown into prison. Perhaps he believed, like the historian, Matthew Paris, that Cynefritha took an active part in the beheading of Ethelbert. She was also believed to have been in league with Winbertus, who, according to an account by the early medieval prior, Osbert of Clare, had been promised half the kingdom for carrying out the deed. Certainly Cynefritha must have been unusually forceful and independent, for coins have been discovered engraved with her name, the only Saxon woman ever to have reached such status.

But, whatever the truth of Cynefritha's involvement, Offa could never have forgotten that he had agreed to the murder of Ethelbert. His daughter, Alfthrytha, was terribly distressed by what had happened and, afterwards became an anchorite, a solitary nun, in an enclosed order at Croyland.

Matthew Paris, a 13th century monk of Saint Albans, wrote a scholarly account of Ethelbert's murder, emphasising Offa's feeling of guilt and deep regret for his evil deed. The story was also told by Giraldus Cambrensis, Gerald of Wales, the Pembrokeshire cleric, who died in 1216 and who was known for his distinguished literary style.

For the remaining two years of his life, Offa's guilt must have constantly haunted him. Yet it was at this time that the construction of the dyke was being completed and surely it is far more for this great achievement, rather than the murder of Ethelbert, that he is remembered. And, though through time much has disappeared, long stretches can still be traced - and walked, mostly following marked footpaths. Along the 1½ miles that run through the parish of Lyonshall there are sections that show clearly how the dyke was constructed. About a quarter of a mile to the south-west of the church follow the footpath towards the south-east and you will find the earthbank with the ditch alongside. In places there are gaps with no sign of dyke or ditch, but then they reappear, sometimes with the earthbank as much as 6 metres high and the ditch close on 4 metres wide - and full in the winter, shadowed under overhanging holly trees and ancient yews.

But perhaps the most beautiful stretch of all is along Hergest ridge to the west of the small town of Kington. There, if you fork left towards Hergest Croft Gardens and follow the lane up the hill, you come to a gate. Beyond it, past a line of enormous beech trees, you are on the Dyke path. And then you can walk and go on walking for mile after mile over springy turf, scattered here and there with clumps of gorse. There are sheep who watch you warily as you pass, shaggy ponies who keep their distance, manes blowing in the wind, and, above you, there are larks, small black specks rising, rising, belting out their high, ecstatic song. And there are views, panoramic, heart-catching views stretching away, ahead, behind, on either side, and constantly changing as you walk. Below in the valleys shadows slide over fields, woodland, scattered farms, and far on the skyline hills emerge, grow, take shape, then further hills...

We cannot thank Offa for the views; they would anyhow have been different then when the landscape was densely forested. But without his dyke the path that follows it would not be there. We can thank him for his dyke.

Saint Augustine's Chair

FOUR MILES FROM BROMYARD, on a hill above the village of Stanford Bishop, is the church of Saint James the Great. It is a peaceful place surrounded by fields and the round churchyard with its massive yew, thought to be 1,200 years old, suggests that the site may have been one of ancient worship. The small stone church is mainly late Norman with some Victorian restoration; it is satisfyingly solid and plain with a broad square tower. There are two windows in the nave of about 1190, there is a Jacobean pulpit, a 13th century font, a 14th century porch. There is also a chair.

It is no ordinary chair; crude, box-shaped, low on the ground, and yet it has a kind of dignity. It looks venerable - and extremely old; the oak is mellowed and smoothed with age.

Old it certainly is, 1,400 years old. If you crouch down and read the brass plaque below the seat you will learn that in 603 AD the great Saint Augustine sat in it - so the story goes. It was the Venerable Bede who, a century later, having studied manuscripts written by the monks of Canterbury, told how Augustine requested a meeting, or synod, with the Celtic bishops to discuss their preaching methods and to synchronise the date for Easter. The Celtic bishops had met Augustine at an earlier synod and found him dictatorial and self-important. Advised by a wise anchorite, a monk from an enclosed order, they decided to test Augustine's humility by arriving at the synod after him. If he stood to welcome them when they arrived it would show that he respected them as equals, that he was lowly of heart, a true follower of Christ. Should he remain seated they would know that he considered them inferior, that he despised them; they should therefore despise him in return.

When the flock of bishops reached Stanford Bishop Augustine was waiting, under an oak tree, in his chair. The bishops approached. Augustine sat - and remained seated; he showed no sign of rising to welcome them. Bede tells how the bishops charged him with being proud and how they refused to confer with him.

Bede, who was born about 675, lived mainly in Durham and Northumbria writing theological, historical and scientific works which were highly respected at the time and have been studied ever since. Which is why he is almost always known as the Venerable Bede.

Augustine's chair, which was apparently kept at Stanford Bishop, was identified by a Doctor James Johnson at the end of the last century. Revisiting the church which he remembered from a childhood holiday, he asked the sexton about the old chair. The sexton explained that the chair had been thrown out during the restoration of the tower and that, as it happened, the workmen, who had lit a fire to brew tea, were about to burn it. Doctor Johnson offered to buy the chair, intending to make it into a garden seat. But, examining it, he discovered that its construction was remarkable. The most intriguing feature was the seat of the chair, which was hinged with round bits of wood called cardines, identical to the type used by Roman carpenters during the time of the Roman Empire. Doctor Johnson, who wrote a book about the chair, concluded that it must have been made before the Roman methods of carpentry had died out in England, some time in the first six centuries A.D.

Doctor Johnson judged the chair too important to keep to himself and for many years it was displayed in the museum in Canterbury. But now it is back where it rightly belongs on the left side of the chancel, a place of honour, in the church of Saint James the Great at Stanford Bishop.

Castles

IT WAS THE NORMANS, a whole millennium after the Iron Age, who built the great stone strongholds of the Borderlands. The word castle, or castellum, was already in use but, confusingly, could mean anything from 'an inhabited place' to a whole town. On the Continent, during the tenth century, the word castellum came increasingly to mean the fortress of a feudal lord. In the next century, as more and more of these strongholds were built in England, the word castle was adopted here.

In some cases the Normans made use of natural hills as sites for their castles, though they rarely seem to have adopted those of the old earthwork forts. Most often they would would choose a new site, throwing up their own artificial mound, or 'motte', surrounding it with a ditch and wall, then building on top. In the Bayeux Tapestry is a picture of King William's troops after the Battle of Hastings throwing up a 'motte'. The inscription reads; 'Jussit ut foderetur castellum' - He commanded a castle to be digged.

The early castles were generally built of timber and typically consisted of a tower with, around it, a palisaded court. On a lower level, below the mound, was a larger court or bailey, also palisaded, and surrounded by a rampart and ditch. Most castles were put up hurriedly to establish a base after a battle; later, when conditions became more stable, the timber would be replaced with stone.

The bailey, sometimes known as the ward, was the open area inside the castle walls. Most castles had an outer and inner bailey, the latter also being referred to as the court, though generally this implied a more confined area enclosed by a stone wall.

° CASTELLVM °

Hereford Castle

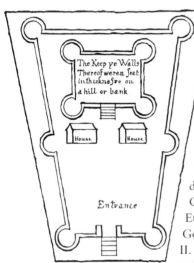

The Keep ye Walls Thereof were ... feet in thickness on a hill or bank

House   House

Entrance

While a prisoner in Hereford Castle, Prince Edward was allowed out under guard to ride on Widemarsh Common. One day, having ridden so hard that his own horse and those of his guards were exhausted, he demanded a fresh mount.

At once he was off, charging at top speed to Wigmore Castle.

THE EARLIEST CASTLE MENTIONED in the Anglo Saxon Chronicle, as something new and remarkable, is at Hereford.

The outline of a castle can still be seen. In hot, dry weather lines begin to appear in the grass on Castle Green, parched brown lines over shallow soil. Below are the foundations of the castle walls. But not of the original castle which would have been far smaller, probably no more than a motte with a tower on top in the north-east corner of Castle Green. This early stronghold was built between 1048 and 1052 by Ralph, Count of Vexin, who in 1046 had been made Earl of Hereford by his uncle, Edward the Confessor. It seems that Earl Ralph, who was reputedly arrogant and overbearing, soon made himself extremely unpopular with both the English and the Welsh. In 1055 the combined forces of the Welsh king, Gruffydd ap Llywelyn, and the Saxon Earl Aelfgar defeated Ralph, destroying the castle, wrecking and burning the city, the Cathedral and, with it, the highly prized bones of saint Ethelbert. Ralph was replaced as Earl of Hereford by Godwin, whose son, Harold Godwinson, became Harold II. Earl Godwin, having chased out the Welsh, built a new wall round Hereford 'fortified with gates and bars and with a broad deep ditch'. It seems he left the castle as it was.

Soon after the conquest William FitzOsbern, the Earl of Hereford, rebuilt the castle, again of timber, on a large motte to the west of Castle Green, joining it to the original motte with an embankment. FitzOsbern was a powerful and effective administrator. In only five years - he was killed in Flanders in 1071 - he strengthened the defences along the Welsh border with a chain of castles including Wigmore, Clifford, Longtown and Kilpeck, he redesigned and expanded Hereford, building a new settlement and market place to the north of the old Saxon defences, the area now called High Town, to encourage trade. And to entice immigrants from his native Normandy he introduced new rules and privileges designed to work to their advantage.

After FitzOsbern's death his son, Roger, was involved in a plot to depose King William. The plot failed but the FitzOsbern estates including Hereford Castle were taken over by the crown.

In the 12th century, during the dispute for the throne between Matilda, the daughter of Henry I, and her cousin, Stephen de Blois, whom the Council of Barons had appointed in her place, the castle changed hands several times. In 1139 Matilda's supporters, Geoffrey Talbot and Milo Fitzwalter, having taken the city, fortified the close, driving out the clergy and billeting their soldiers and horses inside the Cathedral. They succeeded in capturing the castle but not for long. Quite soon it was back in the king's hands. Towards the end of the 12th century the timber structure of the castle was gradually replaced with stone. A massive stone keep was added on the western motte and a collapsing corner tower rebuilt. Bridges were strengthened and the castle walls, particularly the south wall which was continually being undermined by the fast flowing river Wye below. Repairs were ongoing - and expensive. Records show that the £100 spent between 1250 and 1252 was inadequate for all that needed to be done.

Both King John and Henry III often occupied the castle's state quarters which were large and well appointed and supported by kitchens, a counting house, stables, an almonry and two prisons. In 1233 Henry III had a 'fair and becoming chapel' added to his chamber - to pray for victory over Simon de Montfort perhaps, for at that time, the Baron's War was raging on with much of the action taking place round Hereford. A serious setback for Henry was when the Baronial party gained control of the castle, making it their headquarters and imprisoning Prince Edward there. Daringly, while out riding he managed to escape to Wigmore Castle, the home of the Mortimers.

Then quite abruptly in 1282, the situation changed. Following Edward I's conquest of Wales, Hereford Castle was no longer important as a military base. It became neglected. Soon it started to decay. By 1326 when Isabella, the wife of Edward II, visited Hereford, she was housed in the Bishop's Palace. By 1387 the castle was so derelict that Richard II granted the pasture rights to an aptly named Roger Ploughfield. But early in the 15th century the Welsh leader, Owain Glyndwr, led an uprising against Henry IV. The castle was needed as a base again, which meant that work on the structure had to be carried out immediately. There were repairs to the towers and the chapel roof, the rebuilding of the wall above the Wye and a complete reroofing of the great tower.

During the Barons' War the city walls were substantially strengthened. Much of the work was done by the burgesses of the city as, under a Charter issued in 1189, they were required to help with the construction of fortifications.

And that was that. From then on no major repairs to the castle structure were ever undertaken.

During the Civil War, Hereford, a Royalist stronghold, was twice occupied by the Parliamentarians. But in the later stages of the war, the Royalist, Barnabas Scudamore, took charge. He rallied the citizens to mend the defences and take up arms and, right up until Christmas Eve, 1645, the city held out.

After the war Colonel Birch, the Parliamentarian governor of the city, is believed to have organised some work on the castle, though it cannot have amounted to very much, for in 1652 the Surveyor General's report spoke of 'the ruinous castle at Hereford'.

A year later 'a grate part of the stone of the castle' was demolished so that an extension could be added to the Cathedral's College of the Vicars Choral. Soon most of the stonework had been removed and the green then landscaped with paths and walks. In 1809 a memorial to Lord Nelson, who had connections with Hereford, was set in the middle.

The statue is still there as are the paths across Castle Green, the bailey of the castle on its mound, and the moat, a small part of it, the pool beside the Castle Pool Hotel. And, in summer drought, there are lines in the grass.

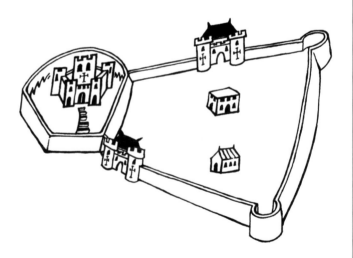

Wigmore Castle

LESS THAN HALF A MILE to the west of Wigmore church are the ruins of a castle. In its day Wigmore was one of the largest of the chain of strongholds along the Welsh border. The original castle, a simple timber construction set on a motte, was built between 1069 and 1071 by William FitzOsbern on what the Domesday Book recorded as waste land. When, in 1075, FitzOsbern's son, Roger, was involved in a plot to unseat King William, the castle was granted to Ralph de Mortimer.

The Mortimers, who had come to England from Normandy at the time of the conquest, were soon to become one of the most powerful families not only in the Borderlands but throughout England. Shrewdly by marriage and land deals they increased their estates, their wealth, their influence. The Mortimers were not always in favour with the Crown. Hugh Mortimer, the son of Ralph, was continually in trouble with Henry II, the first of the Plantagenet kings, mainly because, in the dispute for the throne, he had supported Stephen rather than Henry's mother, Matilda. It was Hugh who, in 1179, founded Wigmore Abbey in the valley about 1½ miles north of the castle. The Augustinian order of the Canons of Saint Victor of Paris, had previously been at Shobdon.

By the end of the 12th century parts of the early timber construction of the castle would have been replaced with stone. It was a process that went on, with further buildings being added, so that by the mid 14th century the castle was probably at its most splendid, fully equipped for defensive warfare as well as noble living. An inventory of the contents taken in 1325 includes crossbows made of horn and wood, siege engines for throwing large stones, lances, spears, chain mail, armour... and, more pleasurably, a chess board with painted and gilded chessmen, a board for drafts, five peacocks and sundry beasts.

In the early 14th century, the young Roger Mortimer, the first to take the title Earl of March, became involved with Queen Isabella, the French wife of Edward II. Together they plotted to get rid of the King and when

Roger, who had been imprisoned in the Tower for armed rebellion, managed to escape, he joined the Queen in France. In 1326, with a small force of men, they landed in England, captured the King and eventually had him murdered in Berkeley Castle. Meanwhile Roger and the Queen, openly lovers, ruled the country until, in 1330, Edward III, ascending the throne, had Mortimer arrested and hanged at Tyburn.

In 1425 Edmund Mortimer, the 5th Earl of March, died without an heir. His estates went to his nephew, Richard Duke of York, a descendant through his mother of Edward III. This was why, three decades later, Richard was one of the leading players in the Wars of the Roses, the thirty year contest for the throne between the houses of York and Lancaster.

Richard was killed at the Battle of Wakefield in December, 1460. His severed head, wearing a paper crown, was stuck up over the city gates. But a few weeks later on a snowy February day his 19 year old son, the 7th Earl of March and the future Edward IV, had his revenge. At Mortimer's Cross near Leominster he met the combined armies of the Earl of Pembroke and Owain Tudor. After a long and bloody battle Edward succeeded in defeating them. Afterwards eight of the top ranking Lancastrians were marched 16 miles into Hereford and publicly beheaded.

After the Wars of the Roses Wigmore Castle was rarely occupied. It had already begun to deteriorate since for several generations the Mortimers had preferred to live in their great stronghold at Ludlow.

Towards the middle of the 16th century Bishop Lee, the President of the Council of the Marches, described Wigmore as 'utterly decayed in lodging', and, though some repairs were done so that for a while it could be used as a prison, security cannot have been very tight.

In 1643, during the Civil War, the Parliamentarians effectively destroyed the outer walls, towers and the gatehouse. Perhaps they judged it too difficult to repair but feared the Royalists might think otherwise. For, despite the decay, with its strategic position and its size, such a stronghold could still have been a worthwhile prize.

The castle stands at the end of a high bluff with a deep ravine, perhaps man made, to both east and west. The main enclosure measures roughly 100 metres by 70 and was surrounded by curtain walls connecting the three main towers. The gatehouse, on the south side, led into the courtyard where the living quarters were built on a raised plateau. Excavations have shown that these were extensive

---

This Pedestal is erected to perpetuate the memory of an obstinate, bloody, and decisive battle fought near this Spot in the civil Wars between the Houses of York and Lancaster on the 2nd Day of February 1461 between the Forces of Edward Mortimer Earl of March (afterwards Edward the Fourth) on the Side of York and those of Henry the Sixth on the Side of Lancaster.

The Kings Troops were comanded by Jasper Earl of Pembroke. Edward comanded his own in Person and was victorious. The Slaughter was great Four Thousand being left dead on the field and many Welsh Persons were taken prisoner among whom was Owen Tudor (Great Grandfather to Henry the Eighth and a Defendent of the illustrious Cadwallader) who was afterwards beheaded at Hereford.

This was the decisive Battle which fixed Edward the Fourth on the Throne of England who was proclaimed King in London on the fifth of March following

---

As young Edward Mortimer moved his troops into battle line at Mortimer's Cross, three suns were seen simultaneously in the sky. Edward, thinking quickly, swung his charger to face the Lancastrians proclaiming it an omen, a sign from God. 'These three suns betoken the Father, the Son and the Holy Ghost. In the name of Almighty God do we march against our enemies.' The battle is commemorated on a large stone set up outside the Monument Inn on the edge of the village of Kingsland.

with large fireplaces and steps leading down to high-ceilinged basements. In the north-west corner a large shell keep standing on its own motte was occupied when the castle was under attack. And, when the situation became desperate, the ultimate refuge was an octagonal tower beyond the shell keep.

Part of the shell keep has survived but the tower beyond it has entirely gone. As has so much else. There are remnants of the towers and the curtain walls, there is the arch of the gatehouse which has sunk right down and is half buried under crumbling masonry. And everywhere, over all that remains, grow bushes, brambles, ivy, trees, as if the castle, once so splendid, the pride of the mighty Mortimers, wanted to conceal its sad decline.

But salvation, or anyhow better times, lie ahead. In 1996 English Heritage became responsible for the site which was fenced off so that a major restoration project could begin. By the end of the century the castle ruins will have been made safe and the site will be open to visitors. Then once more the greatness of the Mortimers can be recalled.

The name Wigmore comes from the shape of the land. The old English word 'wicga', meaning beetle, a wriggling insect, a description of the curve in the high moorland that extends southwards between the Teme and the Lugg.

Ludlow Castle

O F ALL THE CASTLES ALONG the Welsh border Ludlow is generally considered the greatest, the most historically important, the best preserved, the most magnificent.

If all that sounds overloaded with superlatives look at it from Whitcliffe on the Ludford side of the river Teme. It stands on the summit of a wooded cliff, more than 30 metres high, its battlements mirrored in the stream below. Superlatives are in order then.

Set into the outside wall of the Inner Court, close to the well, is a postern or sallyport, a low gateway or escape hatch, generally at the back of a building. There is another in the north wall of the outer bailey. Both are directly above the cliff.

The original stronghold was built at the end of the 11th century, probably about 1085, by Roger de Lacy, one of the leading Marcher lords, on land granted to his father Walter de Lacy, by William the Conqueror. Roger chose a site with a commanding outlook and one which was easily defensible, with both the Teme and its tributary, the Corve below its west and north sides. To defend the south and east a deep dry ditch was quarried out of the natural rock, a chunky siltstone, on which the castle stood. Ingeniously two sections of this stone were left to support the drawbridge on either side. Beyond is the enormous outer bailey surrounded by a wall 3 metres thick with a gate into the town which, at the end of the 11th century, if it existed at all, was no more than a small huddle of houses. In the shadow of de Lacy's stronghold and enclosed within its own protective wall it began to grow, at first as a suburb of the castle, supplying its needs, but later, with the development of the wool trade, becoming a thriving market town.

The groundplan of the castle is roughly square but it is not until you go inside that the layout becomes clear. Once through the entrance gate, you look across the great expanse of the outer bailey to the north-west corner, to the heart of the castle, the inner bailey, surrounded by its ditch and semi-circular wall. It was here, at the edge of the cliff, that Roger de Lacy built his castle, a basic timber structure, far smaller than it grew to be eventually. Later the timber was replaced with stone, possibly the siltstone quarried from the ditch. The other stone used was the local red sandstone, which is generally more suitable for building.

The castle grew in stages, Norman, Medieval, Tudor. The walls surrounding the inner bailey and the gatehouse keep must have been added soon after the original build, early in the 12th century. The keep, massive, four-square and unusually high, combined the gatehouse entrance on ground floor level with living quarters above; the hall, solar and adjoining rooms. Two other early Norman towers are on the south side of the castle; one, set into the south-west corner of the inner court, was later known as the Oven Tower; the kitchens were built to the east of this, close to the well, thought to be 26 metres deep.

Then there is the Norman chapel which was built about 1140 and is dedicated to Saint Mary Magdalene. It is curious, a one-off; it is also enchanting. Standing on its own in the inner bailey, you notice it at once. It is completely round. The roof is missing and the chancel has been pulled down but much of the decoration is still intact; the zigzag pattern over the doorway and the chancel arch, the carved arches round the inside walls and above them on the corbels, the stone projections that possibly supported an upper floor, three faces staring down. And, though no trace of them remains, decorated tiles once covered the floor.

In 1240 the de Lacy line died out and the ownership went to the French de Geneville family. Their most important addition was the north range, which Peter de Geneville began in 1280 and which was later expanded and developed. The finished range with its great hall, passages, basements and stairs leading to many upper rooms, is said to be one of the finest examples of Medieval domestic architecture in the country.

In 1307, when the heiress, Joan de Geneville, married Roger Mortimer, Ludlow became Mortimer territory, a part of it; the Mortimers, a

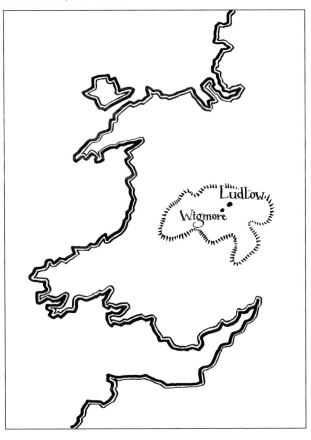

The name LUDLOW comes from two Anglo-Saxon words; 'Lud' meaning 'by the loud waters' and 'low' meaning 'a hill'.

powerful Marcher family, already owned vast areas of land. But they favoured Ludlow which soon replaced Wigmore as their principal seat. And not simply as a stronghold. Roger Mortimer wanted more than that and he set about converting and enlarging the castle into a magnificent palace. As well as the semi-circular Mortimer's Tower on the west side, it was probably Roger Mortimer who built the Chapel of Saint Peter to the east of the gatehouse. Another development sometime early in the 14th century was the alteration of the keep. It was decided that the position of the living quarters above the gatehouse entrance was hazardous. So the south entrance was blocked off and a new one made further to the east. In the 15th century the keep was reduced in size by cutting off a section on the north side.

During the Wars of the Roses the castle reached the peak of its importance. When Richard, Duke of York, a Mortimer descendant, was crowned King of England, Ludlow became a royal palace. It was a particular favourite of Richard's son, Edward IV, whose own two sons lived there until they were sent to London, to the Tower, where they were put to death.

In 1475, when the Council of the Marches was set up to govern Wales and the Borders, Ludlow was chosen as its headquarters and its President had his residence in the castle.

And its greatness continued through the 16th and 17th centuries. Prince Arthur, the elder son of Henry VII, lived there with his bride, Catherine of Aragon, until in April, 1502, he died in the north-west tower, which then became known as Arthur's Tower. Mary Tudor chose to spend the three winters between 1525 and 1528 there. And during the reign of Elizabeth I, Sir Henry Sydney, then the President of the Council of the Marches, added another building to the east of the 14th century gatehouse.

Throughout the centuries life at the castle would have been enriched by music, dance and drama, but one evening in 1634 an entertainment was given that stands out in the castle's history. The first performance of *Comus* by John Milton, a masque with singing and dancing, was staged within the inner court.

During the Civil War there was little serious damage to the structure of the castle and, though during the Commonwealth the Council of the Marches was disbanded, in 1660 it was reinstated. Not for long. Less than three decades later the Council was abolished.

For a time a skeleton company of troops occupied the barracks built against the wall of the outer bailey; otherwise the castle was deserted. And that was how it stayed until the reign of George II, when its upkeep was considered an unjustified expense. The troops moved out, the lead from the roof was stripped off and sold. The stonework crumbled, the roofs fell in. Eventually, in 1811, the ruins were sold to the Earl of Powis.

Now, its buildings made safe and well protected, the castle is open to visitors. Thousands come each year to wander round. In a sense the place is brought to life again. But perhaps what most vividly links the past with the present day is that every summer, as part of the Ludlow Festival, a play is performed in the heart of the castle, in the inner court, a tradition established by Milton's *Comus* more than three and a half centuries ago.

Three Castles

BETWEEN HEREFORD AND MONMOUTH, in the Monnow valley where the river winds between small hills, are the ruins of three castles, Grosmont, Skenfrith and White. Although they are now on the Welsh side of the border, in north Gwent, originally they were part of the chain of strongholds built by the Normans along the boundary between England and Wales to protect their newly conquered lands. Being less than five miles apart these three castles formed a triangle so vital to the defence of the region that only a lord entirely trusted by the king was granted ownership.

Grosmont
Skenfrith
White Castle

All three were originally motte and bailey strongholds built, mainly of timber, at the end of the 11th century, probably by the Earl of Hereford, William FitzOsbern, or by one of his companions. There are few records of their early history but we know that in the 12th century the three castles were in the hands of the Crown, being administered by the Sheriff of Hereford. Towards the end of Henry II's reign, despite an agreement with the Welsh prince, Rhys ap Gruffydd, to keep the peace, the Welsh stepped up their attacks. In 1182 there was the burning of Abergavenny Castle and the assault on Dingestow, six miles from Skenfrith, when the sheriff of Hereford was killed. As a result the defences of each castle were strengthened.

In 1201, King John granted the Three Castles, as they became known, to an officer in his service, Hubert de Burgh. When, four years later, Hubert de Burgh was imprisoned in France, the King transferred ownership to the Lord of Abergavenny, William de Breos. Before long William de Breos had fallen out with the King and lost his lands, and though his sons regained possession, in 1219 the King's Council returned the Three Castles to Hubert de

In Norman England the Justiciar, the office held by Hubert de Burgh, was the chief justice minister, a position second in power only to the King. By 1265 the division of government into different departments such as the Chancery and the Exchequer, meant it was no longer advisable for one man to be in overall charge.

Burgh. By then Hubert had greatly increased his power; he had been one of King John's advisers at the time of Magna Carta in 1215, he had been appointed Justiciar and created Earl of Essex. With the Three Castles once more in his possession he set about rebuilding Grosmont and Skenfrith.

Grosmont, the most important of the three, and in its day the most splendid, is at the northern point of the triangle, close to the Monnow. The castle stands on high ground at the edge of Grosmont village, which is small and peaceful with a church that seems too big for its size. Like the castle, the church, dedicated to a favourite Norman saint, Nicholas of Myra, was rebuilt by Hubert de Burgh.

Opposite the post office in the main village street is a footpath which leads steeply up hill to grazing land. This was once the outer bailey of the castle. Beyond, surrounded by a formidable ditch, are the walls and towers of the castle itself.

A wooden drawbridge would have crossed the ditch to the gatehouse on the south-west side. This was rebuilt in 1330, replacing the smaller original structure; at the same time the gatehouse passage was lengthened allowing for a drawbridge pit. But part of the stone structure, the work of Hubert de Burgh, is more than a century older. Adjoining the gatehouse and extending along the east side of the courtyard is his rectangular Hall Block. It is huge; 29 metres long by 13 metres wide and is divided in two sections, north and south. The hall, on the first floor of the northern end, was reached by outside wooden steps from the court. On an inner wall, the base of a spiral staircase leading to living quarters on the floor above is still visible. The curtain walls with their three projecting drum towers were built about 1230. The south-west tower contains a round basement, below ground level, and three D-shaped upper rooms, but until 1330, when the tower was extended inwards, there were no stairs. It was about that time that all but the basement of the north tower was demolished and a new three story chamber block was built on its east side. These were living quarters where comfort mattered; in each main room was a fireplace. And from them the smoke was channelled up a chimney built above the basement of the old north tower. The chimney has survived. It rises high above the curtain walls, it catches the eye. It is extraordinary. A castle with a chimney; unique, perhaps. And such an elegant chimney, octagonal and with a patterned lantern, the section at the top, to let out the smoke.

Sheltered by its castle, Grosmont grew into a fair-sized town. According to local tradition, in the early Middle Ages it boasted the third largest population in South Wales; only Abergavenny and Carmarthen were greater - which is hard to believe when you go there now.

The 14th century building was the work of the Earls of Lancaster, who had inherited the Three Castles in 1267. For a time, after Hubert de Burgh fell from power in 1239, all three reverted to the crown. Then in 1254 Henry III granted them to his eldest son, Prince Edward, and thirteen years later, transferred ownership to his second son, Edmund Crouchback, Earl of Lancaster.

Grosmont, with its high quality accommodation, was a favourite with the Earls of Lancaster, who used it frequently. This was nothing new; from its earliest days, due to its strategic importance in the defence of the region, the castle was often occupied.

The situation had been particularly serious in the early part of the 13th century when the Welsh prince, Llywelyn the Great, united the forces of the north and south against the English. In 1228, Hubert de Burgh, with the young Henry III, launched an expedition against the Welsh. The expedition failed; it also spurred Llywelyn the Great into fiercer and more frequent attacks.

In 1232 Hubert de Burgh, at odds with the King, lost possession of the Three Castles and was imprisoned in Devizes Castle. The next year he escaped, joined the opposition led by Richard Marshal, the Earl of Pembroke, and that November, when Henry III was in residence at Grosmont, their combined forces sprang a night attack on the King's soldiers camped outside the castle. Taken by surprise the King's men fled into the darkness - so the story goes. Whatever the truth, the castle was not captured.

In time Hubert de Burgh was reconciled to Henry III - up to a point; he never fully won back his former powers nor his influence over the King. And, though once again he regained possession of the Three Castles, it was not for long. In 1239 he was finally forced to surrender them together with his castle at Hadleigh in Suffolk. According to the 13th century chronicler, Matthew Paris, these four were his dearest possessions on which he had spent enormous sums.

At the end of the 13th century, following Edward I's conquest of Wales, the Three Castles lost their strategic importance. Nonetheless Grosmont continued to be popular with the Earls of Lancaster, though towards the middle of the 14th century they used it less and less. In 1362, through his marriage to the Duchess Blanche, John of Gaunt became the Earl of Lancaster. The focus of his interest was a long way east of the Monnow valley. Grosmont, from then on, was rarely used.

Even so, at the start the 15th century two important battles took place at Grosmont. The first was in 1405 when the Welsh leader, Owain Glyndwr, who had launched a

Edward I's conquest of Wales ended with the defeat and death of Llywelyn ap Gruffydd, the last of the Welsh princes. This grandson of Llywelyn the Great had taken advantage of the Baron's War, when the English were feuding among themselves, to extend his power. Two years after his death in 1284, Edward I brought the whole principality under his direct rule. To underline his authority he built a number of new castles in Wales. Two of them, Conway and Caernarvon, are shown on the Hereford Mappa Mundi, which was made at about this time.

rebellion against the crown, laid siege to the castle. Relief came when Prince Harry, later Henry V, arrived on the scene and forced Glyndwr away. The following year, Owain Glyndwr's son, Gruffyd, led another attack. That too failed. Afterwards the Welsh rebellion crumbled. The same was true of Grosmont. Neglected and abandoned, it gradually decayed. By the middle of the 16th century it had become a ruin.

On the west bank of the Monnow, some five miles south Grosmont, is the village of Skenfrith. Unlike Grosmont with its hilltop castle at the edge of the village, Skenfrith's is low lying; it is close to the church and the village pub; it is there, in the middle, the focal point.

The earliest records of Skenfrith Castle were made during the reign of Henry II when the Three Castles were in the hands of the Crown. In 1186 £43 17s 7d was spent on strengthening the defences, which at that stage were probably still earth and timber rather than stone. The work was carried out under the direction of a military engineer, Ralf of Grosmont, and must have been prompted by the escalation of the Welsh rebellion at around that time. Records show that in the next seven years another £21 12s 9d was paid for the repair of palisades and the construction of the bailey, an enormous outlay for work that was destined not to last.

The stone castle, as it stands today, was built almost entirely by Hubert de Burgh between 1228 and 1239. Although he had regained possession of the Three Castles in 1219, his dispute with the sons of William de Breos over ownership was not finally settled till 1228. Before then he is unlikely to have risked embarking on major building work.

The earliest stone construction is probably the curtain wall surrounding the roughly rectangular enclosure and the drum towers at each corner. The wall is 2½ metres thick and has survived remarkably, almost to its original height; though, in places, the upper part of the parapet is missing the wall walk is still there, a narrow pathway along the top with steps up to the roof level of the towers. And, at intervals, on top of the wall there would have been fighting galleries built

When Hubert de Burgh lost possession of the Three Castles in 1232 they were granted to the nephew of Hubert's rival, Peter de Roches, the Bishop of Winchester. Before long both he and his nephew were removed from their positions and a trusted employee of the Crown, Waleran the German, was appointed as custodian. For a time Hubert de Burgh regained possession, but when in 1239 he lost everything, Waleran again took charge. During his second stint as custodian, a period of fourteen years, Waleran spent £6 7s on building a new chapel at Skenfrith and roofing the King's Tower with lead.

of wood projecting outwards over the moat. The corner towers were built to a single plan; each has a circular basement reached only through a trapdoor from above used as a store room or possibly a dungeon, and each has a narrow doorway over 2 metres above ground level leading to the first floor, presumably up wooden steps. The first floor walls have three arrow loops, evenly spaced, two to the sides, one to the front.

In the middle of the west wall is a fifth tower, semi-circular and solid right up to the wall-walk level, one of the few parts not built by Hubert de Burgh. It was added later, probably towards the end of the 13th century to strengthen the defences against the forces of Llywelyn ap Gruffydd. At the mid point of the long east wall steps lead down to a watergate. Beyond is the mill stream diverted from the Monnow which runs beside it, but, as the mill stream is believed to be medieval, in Norman times the river would have flowed past the eastern wall. Around the other three sides a ditch was dug, wide and deep with a 2 metre berm, a stone ledge, between the ditch and the wall. There would, of course, have been a drawbridge across the moat operated from a gatehouse on the north side, very little of which remains.

Hubert de Burgh had great influence over the young Henry III, who had come to the throne in 1216 at the age of nine. Records show that Henry stayed at Skenfrith during September 1221 and again during August of the following year, no doubt with Hubert in attendance.

The gravel from the digging of the moat was tipped inside the walls in order to raise the ground level. When Hubert de Burgh came to build the keep the floor of the court was 2½ metres higher than before and with another 2 metres of gravel built up round its foundations, this great round tower, which measures 6 metres across, appears to stand on its own small hill. The extra height allowed the defenders to shoot from the roof right over the walls. Hubert de Burgh did not finish his keep, designed to contain a basement and two upper floors. Perhaps his fall from power in 1239 interrupted its construction. He must have hated to abandon it; he died four years later before it was completed. That was achieved eventually by Waleran, the German custodian.

In 1954, during excavations, a whole range of buildings came to light on the west side of the enclosure. Hubert de Burgh constructed these before the ground level was raised so that the main rooms are on basement level, reached down a long flight of steps. After winter flooding the north end was downgraded to a cellar; the south end, being slightly higher and provided with a large fireplace, must have continued to be used as a Hall.

After 1244, when Waleran built a new chapel and roofed the keep, the only addition was the fifth tower in the west wall. Apart from that there was no further construction, none at all, no alterations, no repairs even, worth mentioning. Despite extensive rebuilding of Saint Bridget's, the enchanting village church, the castle was not touched. The earls of Lancaster used Grosmont; Skenfrith, it seems, did not interest them.

Although ownership remained with the Duchy of Lancaster right up to 1825, the last Steward of the Duchy to be governor of the Three Castles was John Morgan, who, when he died in 1557, was buried in Skenfrith church. By then, though there is no direct evidence, it is likely that the castle was derelict. Certainly by the early 18th century, according to an engraving published then, it was as ruined as it is today.

White Castle, or Llantilio as it used to be before its 13th century coating of white plaster, is out on its own, in every sense. Signs marking the Three Castles Walk point to White Castle, west from Skenfrith for about five miles, up winding lanes higher and higher to where it stands on a pass across the Skerrid Fawr mountains commanding an enormous view.

Like Grosmont and Skenfrith, Llantilio was built as an earthwork castle at the end of the 11th century. Early in the 12th century Henry I granted the lands of Hugh de Lacy, Lord of Ewyas, which included Llantilio, to Payn FitzJohn. Records show that, in 1137, King Stephen confirmed the passing of these lands to Payn FitzJohn's son-in-law, Roger of Gloucester. It was probably Roger who built the great square keep, the base of which still remains at the south end of the inner bailey.

White is by far the largest of the Three Castles. The outer bailey, a great semi-circle ringed by a ditch, measures roughly 84 metres by 74 metres. To the south the inner bailey, shaped like an egg, stands on a mound about 45 metres long by 35 metres wide, a separate ditch surrounding it. Unlike Grosmont and Skenfrith, residential strongholds lived in by a lord, White was an outpost, a base camp for the garrisoning of soldiers. In its early days the troops were probably housed in timber buildings set against the walls. We know from Henry II's Pipe Rolls, that from 1155 money was spent on maintaining and garrisoning Llantilio, as it was then. Later, between 1184 and 1186, the curtain wall of the inner bailey was built at a cost of £128, a colossal sum in those times.

Hubert de Burgh, who owned the Three Castles from 1201 to 1239, may have been responsible for some rebuilding and, according to records, Waleran, the German custodian, who followed Hubert, built a hall, buttery and pantry in 1244. But it was in the 1260's, when possession of

Saint Bridget's church has a short square tower with a pyramid roof, louvred below to let out the sound of the ringing bells. The tower was also a dovecote, perhaps housing a useful source of food, pigeon pie for the villagers.

The Pipe Rolls were the account records of the Exchequer of England. Each Michaelmas, September 29th, from 1129 right up to 1831, amounts paid into the royal treasury were recorded on long sheets of parchment which, when completed, were rolled up into 'pipes'.

the Three Castles passed to the Earls of Lancaster, that the increased threat to the whole region from the Welsh led by Prince Llywelyn ap Gruffydd, triggered a major remodelling and strengthening of the castle.

Between 1267 and 1277, the early keep was demolished and the curtain wall was fortified by six projecting towers. The northern pair, flanking the gatehouse, are roughly 8 metres in diameter and an impressive 14 metres high. Inside them above unlit basements are round rooms up to the wall walk at the top. The two southern towers are larger still, 10 metres across; they are four stories high. On the ground level of the south-east tower was the chancel of a chapel. Alongside it against the eastern wall were the solar and the hall with the well between. On the west side were kitchens and offices.

At the end of the 13th century, when the Three Castles lost their strategic importance, White was used as an administrative centre by the Earls of Lancaster - for a time. And at intervals troops were garrisoned there - when the need arose. The need decreased. Repairs to the structure were left undone. Soon it started to decay. By the 16th century records show that it was derelict.

But White cannot truly be called a ruin. Walk round the ditch of the inner bailey, look up at the walls, which, except for a section on the east side, have survived up to the wall-walk level and which appear impregnable. Stop and look up at the massive towers, their arrow loops like cut-out swords. Seven centuries on, you still feel their power.

In 1922 the last owner of White Castle, Henry Jackson, gave it to the State for preservation. Like Grosmont and Skenfrith, it is open to the public. Like Grosmont and Skenfrith, it is memorable.

Goodrich Castle

GOODRICH CASTLE IS UNIQUE; it is the only Norman stronghold in Herefordshire which is not a total ruin. Its walls, towers, the Norman keep, stand majestically above the Wye. Coming from the village you suddenly catch sight of it, dark against the skyline, impressive, formidable.

The Normans must have cheered when they found the site; the steep bluff protected by the river on the north and east, the far reaching outlook in every direction, including across hostile Wales, to the south and west. And when they dug out the ditch they struck a bed of rock, a solid base on which to build the motte. From the nearby woods, the Forest of Dean, they would have cut down trees, stalwart oaks, for the construction of the castle, Goodric's Castle, as the first one was called. According to the Domesday Book, the survey carried out in 1086, the original was built by Godric of Mappestone, entirely of timber. In time the wooden structure was replaced by stone. Goodric's wooden stronghold became Goodrich Castle.

The first stone addition was the Norman keep which dates from the late 12th century. It is built of grey stone – all the rest is red sandstone – with an entrance reached by wooden steps which could be removed for safety during an attack. The whole castle is geared for effective defence. You are aware of it at once, as, beyond the outer barbican, you cross the moat – no longer over a wooden drawbridge – into the gatehouse passage. There, not only were there massive oak doors, but a pair of portcullises, which would have been lowered through openings in the roof from the room above. Through smaller openings, the murder holes, missiles would have come hurtling down as well as boiling oil. And, if you turn and look back, high behind you on the outer wall, are arrow loops, strategically placed for shooting an attacker in the back.

But once inside the castle, enclosed within walls of up to 3 metres thick, the sense of danger recedes. You feel shielded from attack, secure even. And, surprisingly, there is a feeling of space. Of course the now empty courtyard would have been filled with timber buildings, mainly living quarters, adding to those inside the Norman keep. But there was room to move around, and on several levels, from the lookouts high on the battlements to the storerooms and dungeons underground.

What strikes you too is that life inside the castle, apart from during battles or a siege, would have been orderly and, increasingly, civilised. When the lord was away the castle constable took overall charge. He lived above the gatehouse passage in one of the two sizeable rooms; the portcullises occupied the other. Beside the gatehouse, the semi-circular chapel tower, contains the 13th century chapel. Its east window of reset 15th century glass, throws light on the sedile, the priest's seat set in the wall beside the altar, which is believed to be older than the castle itself and may have come from the earlier Goodric's Castle. On the west wall a modern window commemorates servicemen and civilians killed while working in radar development from 1936 to 1976.

The most important room is the great hall which measures 20 metres by 9 metres. It lies on the west side of the castle, the safest side, where, below the precipitous cliff, the Wye curves round the base of the motte making it virtually impenetrable. This meant that there could be windows, generous windows, both on the outer and inner walls, so that with a fireplace large enough to roast an ox, the hall would have been light as well as warm. Next to the hall in the south-west tower, the largest of the four, was the pantry and buttery leading to the kitchen with its fireplace, a row of ovens and a sluice for washing. Eventually, instead of water carried from the well, it was piped in from a spring across the valley. That would have also been a bonus in the garderobe tower; inside was the triple-holer loo, with a stone-lined cess pit underneath.

There was another range of buildings on the north side of the courtyard, the living quarters of the lord and his family. In the 15th century the roof was raised and a new floor inserted to provide more rooms.

There are very few records of the early history of Goodrich though we know that through the centuries the castle changed hands several times. In the 12th century from the de Clares of Pembroke it passed to the Marshalls and then, through marriage, to the Valence family. In the 14th century it came into the possession of the Talbots, the lords of Archenfield, who later became the Earls of Shrewsbury. The castle's most famous moment came during the Civil War when it was held by Sir Henry Lingen for the Royalists. One by one every other stronghold in Herefordshire fell to the Parliamentarians. Only Sir Henry Lingen held firm. Then in 1646, not long before the end of the war, a force of Parliamentarians under Colonel Birch laid siege to Goodrich. For four months they bombarded it continually.

During that time Charles Clifford, a Royalist soldier defending the castle, sent secret messages to Colonel Birch's niece, Alice. They had met at some time before the siege and fallen in love. One stormy night Clifford managed to escape from the castle and make his way through the besieging force to where Alice was waiting with a horse. Their only route to safety was across the Wye. In torrential rain Clifford forced the horse into the surging water. They did not get far. All three were swept away and never seen again.

Soon afterwards Colonel Birch brought up batteries of cannon, among them Roaring Meg, a particularly fearsome weapon, which was aimed towards the south wall of the Castle. The firing began; alarmingly soon the wall was breached. And, judging all hope lost, Sir Henry Lingen surrendered.

The actual damage caused by Meg was comparatively slight. Certainly, now, it is hard to detect any sign of it in the massively buttressed walls. But the Parliamentarians did not stop there. They stormed the Castle, wrecking the whole interior, reducing the building to an empty shell.

For nearly three centuries Goodrich was abandoned. Weeds and brambles grew unchecked, birds, small animals and ghosts made themselves at home. Then in 1930 the authorities took over, first the Ministry of Works then English Heritage. The site has been cleared and safely fenced; there is a well-kept path leading from the car park and picnic area to the ticket office by the barbican. Thousands of visitors come each year. Which, of course, is right.

But if perhaps you feel that something of the atmosphere has been lost, go down to the Wye below the castle on a stormy night. There, above the noise of the wind and the river, you may catch the sound of a neighing horse, of voices crying out, faint, growing fainter, fainter still ...

Roaring Meg was made at the forge in Whitchurch, not far from Goodrich. Now in Hereford outside Churchill Gardens Museum in Venn's Lane, she looks surprisingly small.

Peterchurch

NO ONE CAN BE SURE when Christianity first spread to Britain. Fourteen centuries ago Pope Gregory sent Augustine from Rome to convert the Anglo-Saxons. But Augustine's mission was not the first. In 563 Columba, the Irish abbot born in Donegal, sailed from Ireland to Iona in the Hebrides. From there, where he founded his famous community, he spread Christianity through Scotland, then south to Britain. Columba had been converted by Patrick, the Roman Briton, who, having escaped from slavery - he had been captured by pirates as a youth - travelled round Ireland preaching the Christian faith. In the north, in the kingdom of Northumbria, the Roman, Paulinus, was probably the earliest Christian missionary. And after him came Aidan, the barefoot saint, who established a community on Lindisfarne.

But long before all these, at the start of the very first century, so the story goes, two of the apostles, Peter and Paul, on parole from their imprisonment in Rome, travelled

first to Spain preaching Christ's word and then sailed north. They landed on the coast of Gwent and continued north to the Black Mountains to the place named Bwlch-yr-Efengyl, the Gospel Pass. There they separated, Paul heading westwards, Peter, south-east to the Borderlands. In the Golden Valley, at Peterchurch, where Peter stopped to rest, he discovered a spring. Having blessed it, he used the water for baptising those he converted. One day a large fish appeared in the hallowed spring, which Peter secured with a golden chain. (Another version of the story tells how Peter placed the fish in the spring to mark it as a holy place.) How long the fish remained in the spring, how long Peter stayed in Peterchurch, what happened to Paul, to both of them before they returned to their martyrdom in Rome, the story does not tell. But, if you think it sounds too tall to be believable, go to Peterchurch, to Saint Peter's parish church. On the wall of the nave, close to the door, on a plaster panel, is Saint Peter's fish, from the look of it more carp than trout but wearing round its neck a golden chain. The panel is dated 1825; it must surely replace one first put up long, long before.

Apart from Peter's fish, the large Norman church is known these days for the height of its spire. From far in the distance, it gleams like a needle against the sky. It is made of fibreglass. Some 50 years ago the 14th century stone spire was taken down; it was replaced in the 1970's with the present one. Sideways on, the church appears to be in four parts, five if you count the tower and spire at the western end. Next is the nave then the chancel divided in two and then the semi-circular apse. The roof height of each part goes down in steps from nave to apse; between each, inside the church, is a rounded arch. Facing east from the west end of the nave you look through three arches of diminishing size to the east window above the altar. The impression is of distance, a far off sanctuary under the sky. For the ceiling of the apse is painted blue, a deep, heavenly kind of blue, and it is studded with stars.

Llanthony Priory

DEEP IN THE BLACK MOUNTAINS between Hay on Wye and Abergavenny is the Ewyas Valley. It is rugged country, beautiful and wild with the Afron Honddu, a tributary of the Usk, winding through the valley which, ringed by the Hatterall Hills, is cut off from the rest of the world. At the end of the 11th century, when the Lord of Ewyas was Hugh de Lacy, the area was swampy and densely wooded; it was easy to get lost.

Which is apparently what happened to the Norman knight, William de Lacy, a kinsman of the Lord of Ewyas, when he went hunting there. Eventually, close to the river, he came upon the remains of a 6th century hermitage believed to have been founded by Saint David himself. The place had a profound effect on him, its beauty, its link with the past, its tranquillity. He decided to change his life, to remain at Llanthony devoting his time to religious contemplation and to rebuilding the little chapel of Saint David. An anonymous 12th century monk tells how William 'dismissed his attendants and hounds and repaired to the cell of Saint David'. But, although he had entirely abandoned his role as a knight at arms, he wore his armour, wore it continually until he died,

so the story goes. Perhaps its weight served as a self-imposed penance, or perhaps, in the damp valley, it was simply that the metal had seized up with rust.

In time, word of William's lonely existence reached the outside world and in 1103 he was joined by a priest called Ernisius, one time chaplain to Queen Maud, the wife of Henry I. Together they decided to establish a monastic settlement on the site of Saint David's hermitage and, with a small band of followers and funds provided by Hugh de Lacy, they set about the rebuilding of the church. By 1108 it was ready to be consecrated by the bishops of Llandaff and Hereford. It is unlikely, however, that the new community was fully established until about 1118. Archbishop Anselm of Canterbury, probably with an eye to increasing the influence of the English church in Wales, took a keen interest in Llanthony, giving advice on its organisation. Ernisius was elected prior and a number of canons were appointed, ordained priests who, as well as taking services at Llanthony, travelled to churches round the countryside. They were known locally as the Black Canons from the colour of their habits.

Llanthony became an Augustinian house, the first in Wales to adopt the Rule. These guidelines, set out by Augustine, were flexible enough to allow, in the remoteness of Llanthony, much of the day to be spent in contemplation. Gerald of Wales, described the monks as 'sitting in their cloisters, breathing fresh air while gazing at distant prospects, mountain peaks rising to meet the sky...' Even in summer there were days when the peaks were capped with snow. The climate was harsh; 'boisterous' was Gerald's word for it. Yet the monks presumably welcomed the cold and unrelenting damp, in theory anyhow, as part of their chosen 'hair shirt' existence. In fact Llanthony was soon widely known and admired for the austerity of its monastic life.

Although at that stage the buildings were smaller and more basic than the present ruins, they covered a wide area and, with the surrounding orchards and gardens, the Priory must have been a remarkable sight, an oasis of order in the wild valley. Roger, Bishop of Salisbury, described it to Henry I as 'the cloister of the mountains'.

But Llanthony owned lands beyond the mountains, mainly Herefordshire estates and farms given by their patron, Hugh de Lacy. Initially William and Ernisius were reluctant to accept such largesse; they were not in the business of acquiring wealth. But realism prevailed and, after all, in justification, money could be used to the glory of God. Another benefactor, Lord Herbert, granted 'the Prior and his Canons' free pasture for their horses throughout all his lands in Wales; they were also invited to fish in the mere. The mere, the Tal y Lyn Pool, known today as Llangorse, is the largest lake in Wales. The path used by the monks, a ten mile hike over the mountains between Llanthony and Langorse, is there today.

The Priory's most illustrious benefactors were Henry I and Queen Maud and Llanthony flourished during their

Among the scandals that shook the Priory in the 14th century was the conviction for theft of one of the canons, John of Hereford, in 1330. He was lodged in the Bishop's prison. In 1376 Prior Nicholas de Timbrey was attacked by three canons while saying prayers for the dead and had his eyes gouged out.

reign. By 1121, when Ernisius retired, there were about 40 canons and 40 monks. Ernisius's successor, Robert de Bethune, apparently grew so fond of Llanthony, that after ten years as prior, he was unwilling to take up his new appointment as Bishop of Hereford until ordered to do so by the Pope.

But there was always, in the background, the threat of attack from the hostile Welsh, and when, in 1135, Henry I died, the rebels took advantage of the turmoil caused by the feud between Stephen and Matilda over the succession, to step up their assaults on the English. The Priory was an easy target. When the Welsh broke in, plundering and killing, canons and monks, led by the prior, fled to Hereford where Bishop Robert de Bethune gave them shelter.

But a few brave canons refused to leave. Even when a Welsh tribal chief is said to have installed himself in the Priory church and held drunken orgies with revels and dancing, they stuck it out, perhaps hiding in the undercroft beneath their quarters praying to be spared. Which apparently they were, for an early record notes that at no time was the church at Llanthony 'wholly deprived of the residence of some of the religious'.

By the spring of 1137 Robert de Bethune had organised an alternative house for the canons in meadows near Gloucester, safely distant from the Ewyas valley. Initially Llanthony Secunda, as it was known, was seen as the daughter house to the Welsh Llanthony, where as soon as conditions were normal again, all the canons would return. But the violence went on and, despite the unsuccessful attempts by Clement, the 5th prior, to introduce compulsory part time residence at Llanthony Prima, most of its possessions – books, vestments, relics, bells, everything of value, were carried off to Gloucester; even the annual revenues were transferred there. Llanthony Secunda took on the status of mother house while Llanthony Prima, increasingly neglected, was used to house the old and infirm, even as a prison, 'a dungeon and a banishment for criminals'.

Quite suddenly some forty years later the fortunes of Llanthony Prima changed. Hugh de Lacy, a descendant of the first patron, was rewarded for his services during Henry II's campaigns in Ireland with grants of lands in Meath, generous grants which he passed on to Llanthony Prima. This welcome injection of funds allowed for repairs and restoration, for building additional monastic quarters, most importantly, for the construction of a great abbey church on the north side of the Priory. This was begun in 1175 and when, in 1230, it was finally completed, it replaced the church rebuilt by William and Ernisius, which later became the infirmary.

It was about this time that the administration of the two Priories was reorganised. The possessions were divided equally and, in 1205, Prima and Secunda were formally separated. Each had a prior, each managed its own affairs. Llanthony Prima flourished again and probably more then than at any other time in its history.

But towards the end of the century debts began to mount. Records show that by 1276 the situation was so grave that Llanthony Prima was taken into royal custody. There was further disruption in the years that followed, when, during Edward I's Welsh campaigns, the Priory was often under attack; several canons were killed, the prior injured. After the conquest, in 1284, Archbishop Pecham toured the monasteries of Wales. He found much to correct at Llanthony Prima. A century on he would have found the same.

Then at the start of the 15th century, during the uprising led by Owain Glyndwr, Welsh rebels occupied the Ewyas Valley. Llanthony Prima was surrounded. Collecting revenues was difficult and dangerous. Living conditions grew worse and worse. Even when the rebellion was over it seems the Priory never fully recovered its former standing.

By 1481, when Edward IV transferred Llanthony Prima's benefices to the Gloucester house, the comparative value put on the two houses, £748 for Llanthony Secunda against £90 for Llanthony Prima, shows how sadly the Welsh house had declined.

And then the Dissolution of the Monasteries; the end for both houses came on March 10th, 1538. In Wales the buildings were demolished, Prior David, his four canons and the few remaining monks were brusquely dismissed. What happened to them then? Was their promised pension of £8 ever paid? We know only that the Priory lands and possessions were sold to the Chief Justice of Ireland, Nicholas Arnolde, for £160. Later the property was bought by the Harley family who, in 1790, sold it to a Colonel Wood of Brecon.

The Colonel had his eye on the area's sporting potential; there were prolific grouse on the surrounding hills. So a lodge for shooting parties was his plan. He converted the south tower at the west end of the abbey, fitting it out to accommodate his guests. He also filled in the high pitched medieval roof on the south side of the tower over the original prior's quarters. This was turned into a house for his steward.

In 1792 the landscape painter, Joseph Turner, visited Llanthony. He painted the view from the south - with artistic licence.

Landor was famously temperamental. He was expelled from Rugby, rusticated from Trinity College Oxford, then fought in Spain as a volunteer against the French. He later lived for many years in Italy, mainly in Florence, where he wrote poetry and drama based on classical models. His work was admired by Robert Browning.

In the 1920's the artist, Eric Gill, with his community of craftsmen and artists, established themselves at Capel y Ffin.

When the Priory next changed hands in 1807 the stonework had deteriorated badly and a considerable amount had been carted away. The new owner, the poet, Walter Savage Landor, somewhat unfairly blamed the Colonel. With no interest in grouse, he intended to pull down the Colonel's lodge, which, as he wrote to his friend, the Poet Laureate, Robert Southey, who lived nearby, so 'shamefully disfigured the ruins'.

Landor made plans, extensive and ambitious plans; to restore the abbey, develop the surroundings, plant a million trees, build a house for himself, a bridge across the river, improve the road ...

Somehow all this did not quite work out. Perhaps if he had spent more time on site overseeing the work, had not employed architects who, as he wrote to Southey, turned out to be 'one great scoundrel followed by a greater', his building projects might have been achieved. But he lived there for less than nine months altogether

On his last visit in 1811, when he brought his wife, Julia, from Italy, he found his tenants had not paid their rents. He confronted them and there were angry, even violent, scenes. He had no time for Welshmen. The feeling was apparently mutual; they allegedly uprooted his newly planted trees. Yet some survived; beech, chestnut, larch, though not the cedars from Lebanon, nor the flock of Merino sheep he imported from Spain. The whole project was vastly expensive. Eventually, a fortune out of pocket, disillusioned, bitter, parted from his wife, he abandoned Llanthony and went back to Florence, to poetry and prose.

It was soon after Landor's death in 1864 that an anglican deacon, Father Ignatius Lyne, attempted to buy the Priory from Landor's son, Arnold, who had inherited the estate. For some time Father Ignatius had longed to restore the Priory and establish a Benedictine community there. The current use of the old Prior's house as a hostelry shocked him deeply and was an added incentive. An unexpected donation enabled him to make an offer. Arnold Landor refused to sell, repeatedly, categorically. Eventually Father Ignatius bought 34 acres of land nearby at Capel y Ffin and offered to exchange it for the four acres where the Priory stood. The answer was the same. So in 1870 Father Ignatius built his monastery at Capel y Ffin. It was known as Llanthony Tertia.

There is still a hostelry – or rather, a restaurant and bar in the undercroft of the old prior's house, with a small hotel in the shooting lodge. And all around the ruins is well-kept grass tended by Cadw. Tourists come, throngs of them in summer. Llanthony is well known.

Yet each time it takes you by surprise; winding along the narrow road, sighting it suddenly, the ruined abbey, dark against the hillside. It lifts your heart.

What strikes you is its size, how it would have looked in medieval times with its twin towers flanking the west entrance, its 8 bay nave and central tower, then 9 metres higher, rising out of the valley, which was far, far wilder and more remote than it is today.

Of the stonework that has survived, outstanding are the arcades, the series of graceful, pointed arches, typical of the late 12th and early 13th centuries, which divide the three nave aisles.

To the east of the nave the central tower over the canons' choir was supported on four massive arches. Now, since so little of them remains, a modern buttress takes their place. The transepts, projecting on either side, form the crossing – or did so once; the north transept, thought to have been damaged by attack before the Dissolution, is no longer there. At the east end of the Abbey are three bays of the presbytery and, on the north side, one round-headed lancet window. Once there were twelve, six each side, and once, as an 18th century engraving shows, there was a large east window with fine tracery above the altar.

To the north and south of the presbytery were small chapels, probably two on each side, dating from about 1177. Excavations of the north chapels in 1978-79 show that the original pair were replaced at different stages by single chapels of varying size. Each time the floor level was raised by deposited rubble from the preceding build. A large rounded arch leads from the south transept to the adjoining chapels. It is believed to be a replacement for two smaller rounded arches. This mix of rounded and pointed arches is a feature of what is known as the Transitional style, the Norman giving way to the Early English. Llanthony Abbey is one of the earliest examples of this style in Wales, possibly the earliest of all. Considering its extreme remoteness such innovation is specially remarkable.

To the south of the abbey, tucked in between the wall of the south transept and the chapter house, is the best preserved of the monastic quarters. The slype, a vaulted passageway, leading from the cloister through to what was probably the cemetery, was where the monks were allowed to meet and talk. Beside it in the large chapter house the prior and canons assembled for instruction, readings and meetings. Being three bays long with a half hexagonal east end there was no shortage of space. Sadly only fragments of the wall shafts have survived. And all that remains of the refectory, which stood at the south end of the cloister, has

On April 5th, 1870, the diarist Francis Kilvert, then curate of Clyro, walked up the lane from Capel y Ffin and saw two Benedictines, black-habited and cowled, digging a garden near the foundations for Llanthony Tertia. Further on, beside the ruins of Llanthony Prima, to his horror he found a pair of tourists, anathema to Kilvert. His next visit to the old Priory was on Midsummer day, rent day. Mrs Beauchamp at the hostelry was too busy preparing the tenants' dinner to provide a meal for Kilvert and his companion. She did however manage 18 eggs, bread, cheese, beer.

In 1837, on Ash Wednesday, 3 piers supporting the south arcade suddenly collapsed. Colonel Wood was unharmed; he was safely in the lodge, eating dinner.

been incorporated into the present wall. Further south were the kitchens and offices and, beyond them, the reredorter, or latrines. The site is now the car park - with lavatories. Some years ago a tunnel discovered there was thought to be a subterranean passage under the mountains. In fact it was the Priory sewer. Beyond the car park was a brewhouse, a dovecote, possibly a guesthouse, and surrounding it all, enclosing it, was a protective wall. Across the fields to the west, and still visible, are the ruins of the gatehouse, the only way in to Llanthony Prima.

Close to the present entrance is the church of Saint David, perhaps the most important building of all, for without it the Priory might never have come into being. It has been beautifully restored and now services are held there regularly.

Inside beyond the arch leading to the chancel, light filters through two round arched windows behind the altar. The stillness is extraordinary.

Or perhaps it is understandable. It has after all been a holy place for fifteen hundred years.

Abbey Dore

I N THE SOUTH-WEST CORNER of Herefordshire, where the Dore river runs through the Golden Valley, is a remarkable building. Its walls are pinkish sandstone, its roof is tiled, it has a strong, square tower. It is Dore Abbey.

Its size, its stature, take you by surprise; it has the air of a cathedral, a magnificence you don't expect to find in a village church. For that is what it is, Saint Mary's, the parish church of Abbey Dore.

Its role has changed. Once it was the centre of a monastery.

Dore Abbey was founded by Cistercian monks in 1147 on land granted by Robert, Lord of Ewyas Harold, one of the leading Marcher lords and a grandson of Earl Ralph, who built Hereford Castle. Robert's own castle at Ewyas Harold, one of the most important of the Border strongholds, was close enough to the Abbey to act as a defensive shield during the many years of fighting between the English and the Welsh.

The Cistercians had come into being in 1098 when Robert, Abbot of Molesme, a Benedictine community near Langres in north-east France, decided to found a more austere and disciplined order. With twenty brother monks he travelled south to the province of Burgundy and there, in the wild forest at Citeaux, he established his new rule. Life for these first Cistercians, who took their name from the area, was exceedingly hard. But that, they believed, was as it should be. Their aim was to follow as closely as possible the way of Saint Benedict himself, dividing their time between prayer and manual labour to keep a balance between mind and body. They wore white to symbolise purity, their buildings were basic and unadorned, they ate no meat.

In time others joined them including Bernard, Saint Bernard, as he was to become. A dynamic and inspirational man, Bernard's influence had a profound effect on the religion, literature and politics of Medieval Europe. In 1114 he founded a new community at Clairvaux and from then on Cistercian houses sprang up all over Europe. By 1164 three hundred communities had been established. By the end of the century there were 694.

Attached to each community were a number of lay brothers, local peasants who acted as unpaid labourers allowing the choir monks time for their routine of religious study and devotion. The lay brothers, who wore brown habits, lived separately, sometimes in granges in the surrounding countryside which in time developed into farms. The Cistercians were agricultural pioneers employing new and more productive methods of cultivation. And they diversified; they grew vines, kept bees, fished, milled flour. (At Dore the corn mill was harnessed to the leat, which doubled as the main drain and which flowed from the nearby river Dore.) They were also pastoral farmers and, particularly in Britain, it was the production of wool which proved their most successful, and profitable, enterprise. By the middle of the 13th century the Cistercians controlled over half the English wool trade.

Inevitably their prosperity led to criticism. They were accused of underhand property deals, of eating meat, of extorting money from the rich, of simply being rich. In fact, records show that the Cistercians never owned enormous wealth. The most serious allegations came from the famously critical 12th century cleric, Gerald of Wales. Possibly his belief that the Cistercians had frustrated his ambition to become the Bishop of Saint David's had something to do with it.

The first Cistercians to come to Britain settled at Waverley in Surrey in 1128. Four years later two communities, Fountains and Rievaulx, were founded in Yorkshire, followed in the next twenty years by some forty more, both monasteries and nunneries, spread throughout England and Wales. The spread was not haphazard. The Cistercian Order, controlled by a General Chapter, was organised into five families each headed by a founding mother house controlling a number of cells or daughter houses. An annual inspection of every daughter house was carried out by the abbot of the mother house. In fact from top to bottom the Cistercian Order was effectively interlinked.

Dore was a daughter house of Morimond, a community on the border between France and Lorraine. Why Robert, the founder of Dore, chose a remote site close to the Welsh

Revenues from wool dropped sharply following the Black Death in 1348, when the labour force was so decimated that, for many years, the few lay brothers joining the order were unable to keep up the previous level of production.

border, may have been due to the Second Crusade. Both happened in 1147. It seems that Robert of Ewyas, who took part in the crusade, may have met monks from Morimond on his way to the Holy Land. Perhaps he spent a night at the Abbey en route – paying guests were a useful source of revenue. Certainly Abbot Rainald of Morimond and Bernard of Clairvaux believed in the crusades. Perhaps they suggested the idea, another 'border' abbey like Morimond. In any case that spring – it was probably on April 25 – Dore Abbey was founded.

Every Cistercian community was required to have a minimum of 12 monks and an abbot. There is no known record of the first monks at Dore, their names, where they came from, nor of their monastery, which they probably built of local timber. Nor are there any records of life during the early years, the period up to the abbacy of Adam I, which began in 1186.

It was during the 30 years of his rule that much of the stone abbey was built; the presbytery, the crossing, the north and south transepts and probably part of the nave. The overall design followed the recognised Cistercian plan; a long nave with narrow aisles, aisleless transepts and presbytery. The high altar was required to be in a square-ended sanctuary, there was to be no figurative sculpture, no elaborate carving, no stained glass. Adam, a strong abbot and reputedly shrewd and ambitious, also built the polygonal chapter house, the

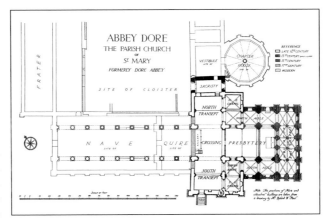

first of its kind in England. Now, where it stood, sheep graze under gnarled apple trees.

Through most of the next century the abbey with its adjoining buildings, the cloister, refectory, sacristy, vestibule, continued to grow. So too did its wealth and influence. There were gifts and grants of land from rich patrons. Many local nobility were buried there. At the end of the 13th century the Bishop of Hereford, Thomas Cantilupe, came to Dore to consecrate the completed abbey – at great risk to his life, the story goes. It seems the Bishop of Saint David's, insisting vehemently that Dore was in his diocese, sent armed soldiers to waylay Thomas Cantilupe. Perhaps, warned, he took another route. Whatever the truth the consecration did take place.

But there were troubles at Dore, increasing as time went by. Corruption was reported, extravagance, the embezzlement of money and valuables – there was a custom for monasteries to act as bankers. One 16th century abbot, John Langdon, is said to have enjoyed hunting, also dishes flavoured with saffron, then a rare, imported spice. In 1524 John Glyn, expelled for misrule from a monastery in Wales, took over as abbot of Dore. And proceeded to squander its resources.

It all ended twelve years later with the Dissolution of the Monasteries. The following spring, on March 1st, Saint David's day, 1537, Dore Abbey was closed down. The last abbot, John Redbourne, was promised a pension of £13 a year, which he never received. And while records show that four of the monks were given payment, the rest, with the lay brothers, were simply dismissed. The land and titles were granted to John Scudamore of Holme Lacy, who was also appointed by the Crown as Particular Receiver. At the sale of goods which took place soon afterwards, he bought most of the household equipment. For £2, a bargain even then, he bought the Abbey roof, the slates and timber of the refectory. Other bargains were the glass and iron from the windows of the dormitory, the refectory and the chapter house. Scudamore bought the lion's share. The beautiful abbey, desecrated and abandoned, lay open to thieves, to wind and rain. But it wasn't abandoned entirely. For the next hundred years, until its restoration was begun, the local people continued to worship there.

The story goes that after the Dissolution, when services were held in the Abbey during wet weather, the parson would stand underneath an arch to keep his prayer book dry.

In 1634 John Scudamore's great grandson, Viscount Scudamore, also John, began the restoration of the eastern arm of Dore Abbey. The nave and all the surrounding buildings had been reduced to crumbling ruins. His decision to go ahead with this major undertaking had been influenced by Archbishop Laud. William Laud was a friend of John Scudamore and his wife, Elizabeth. He used to stay with them and, despite the difference in their ages – Laud, a father figure, was 28 years older – his letters to John Scudamore, particularly those written after the death of five of their infant children, show the closeness of their relationship. It seems that at some point Laud had intimated to John Scudamore that his estates at Lanthony and Gloucester as well as Dore, all once church land, still, according to divine law, belonged to God, that to own them was a sin. For which, John Scudamore came to believe, he was being punished by his infants' deaths. So the Dore restoration was an act of expiation, the price he was paying for his sin.

I had rather be a door keeper in the house of my God: then to dwell in the tents of ungodliness.

The layout of the refurbished abbey reflected Laud's religious views. He believed strongly in man's free will, that salvation was open to everyone. The Calvinists, in contrast, a powerful influence at that time, preached predestination, that only those chosen would be saved. For Laud, who linked his beliefs to ritualised worship, the position of the altar was of prime importance. Lord Scudamore therefore moved the monks' great stone altar with its five carved crosses back to the east end of the chancel beyond the communion rail.

Above it is the east window built by Abbot Adam, triple lancet windows so beautiful they stop you in your tracks. The Cistercian glass was plain. Lord Scudamore's window has stained glass. This was controversial, for since the reformation its use in churches was condemned as idolatrous, Popish, superstitious. But again Scudamore had been influenced by Laud, who believed that stained glass dignified the altar. The Dore window depicts the Ascension with four apostles and the evangelists on either side. Lord Scudamore chose a design in an early medieval style, in keeping with Abbot Adam's time. The glazier is unknown; his bill was £100.

Behind the chancel is the ambulatory, a feature which began to appear in Cistercian churches from the end of the 12th century, with, beyond it, the east chapels, five bays divided by low walls. Lying in these chapels are stone fragments, believed to be mostly from the nave; pieces of tracery, of arches, sections from the destroyed rood screen, and amongst it all, three lifesize heads, which, once on bosses high in the nave, now stare upwards. One, a green man, symbolises the Cistercians' affinity with nature.

As far as possible stone salvaged from the ruined nave was used in the restoration. There were also small pieces of the medieval floor tiles which could be matched to those in the presbytery. Generally however new material was used, stone, locally quarried, and oak, well seasoned, from Lord Scudamore's woods.

The carpenter employed by Lord Scudamore was John Abel, a skilled craftsman who was responsible for all the woodwork of the restored church; the presbytery roof, both the structure and the flat ceiling with its mouldings and carvings, the interior of the tower including the bell frame for six bells, the pulpit, the screen. John Abel's screen is a masterpiece. You notice it at once, dark and magnificent, spanning the eastern side of the crossing. It is five bays wide with a carved frieze and above, between finials, three coats of arms, Royal Stuart flanked by Scudamore and Canterbury.

According to the 18th century historian, Matthew Gibson, long before the restoration the altar had been used for the salting of meat and making of cheese. Later it became buried under rubble until eventually scavengers 'carrying a great deal of Stone away for Common-Uses' revealed it.

The oak gallery set against the west wall of the abbey was added later, probably about 1660.

To the right of the main door of the Abbey is the Hoskyns chapel. Among the memorials to members of this distinguished family is the tomb of John Hoskyns, Serjeant-at-Law and twice M.P. for Hereford during the reign of James I. He was an outstanding scholar, musician and orator and one of the most admired poets of his time. When he died in 1638, of gangrene of the leg, he was buried in Dore Abbey. On the sides of his tomb latin verses pay tribute, in translation, to 'Hoskyns, a prodigy of human genius... Mighty in both Muses and the Law... .'John Aubrey, the 17th century writer, attributes the verses to Hoskyn's friend, Thomas Bonham, the poet John Donne, also, possibly, Hoskyn's son, Bennett.

Outside, John Abel also built the timber-framed south porch which became the main entrance leading into the south transept. On the west side the mason, David Adams, constructed a new wall, blocking off the site of the original nave. His other major work was the great square tower which, according to documents in the Hereford Record Office, was '80 ft. to roof, battlements to go 4 ft. higher... Walls 5 ft. thick to first level'. There was also the renewing of the chancel roof and the 'Body of the church to be covered with Tiles'.

The restoration took two years. On Palm Sunday, March 30th, 1634, the reconsecration took place. It was John Scudamore's birthday. He must have felt immensely proud. Perhaps he also felt forgiven.

At the end of the 19th century Rowland Paul, an art historian with a special interest in monastic architecture, found Dore Abbey badly in need of repair. The whole building was so damp that chunks of plaster ceiling were breaking off and falling; the belfry was positively dangerous. An appeal raised a fraction of the money needed, but enough to make a start. Rowland Paul went ahead, repairing the decay, installing a heating system and, most rewardingly, stripping off whitewash to reveal wall paintings on the south, west and north walls. A great many came to light, in fact, there are thought to be more medieval wall paintings at Dore than any other Cistercian church in England. The clearest are probably around the south aisle and the ambulatory where colour can be seen on arches and pillars. And Paul's research uncovered clues which showed that the nave, its walls and ceiling, had been brightly painted, that the overall impression inside the abbey was of a richness of colour and design entirely different from today's pale stone and remarkably so from the austerity of the earlier Cistercian church. Externally too traces of white mortar confirmed that the walls must have been limewashed. The entire abbey, huge and impressive in its green valley, was gleaming white.

There are also wall paintings that date from the 17th century; the figure of death leaning on his spade in the south transept, 'Time' with his hourglass and scythe close to the blocked arch of the south nave aisle, as well as numerous texts, some legible still.

Outside, Paul discovered more of the medieval floor tiles, some heraldic, some lozenge-shaped with a green glaze and a flower design. Having pieced them together he laid them in the chancel beside the altar. He also retrieved and reset fragments of medieval glass. An example of this is in the Hoskyns chapel to the south-east of the south transept.

Rowland Paul's restoration - the presbytery was reopened in 1904 - added another layer to the history of Dore.

You feel this when you go there, the sense of moving back and back in time. Perhaps it is the height inside the building, the feeling of space, the light through lancet windows. Their shape, the gothic arch, is everywhere. Along the north and south aisles and in the ambulatory to which they lead are vaulted ceilings, echoing the shape. The view through triple arches behind the altar is of further arches and lancet windows in the chapels beyond. So you are always catching glimpses of another place - and another time? And in the east corner of the north transept is a low doorway, a secretive-looking, round-headed doorway. It leads to the sacristy, the room where the monks kept their sacred vessels. Somehow you expect it to be there still.

Partly it is. When you explore outside behind the north wall of the abbey you come first to the sacristy. Roofless now and the floor is grass but the walls are there and on the west side is a recess with moulded stones.

Rowland Paul did extensive detective work on the layout of the monastic buildings. Afterwards he drew out a plan which shows that to the north of the sacristy was the vestibule, a low room with stairs to a dormitory above. Adjoining the vestibule on the eastern side was the chapter house, to the west was the large square cloister court with the kitchens and refectory beyond. Now there is nothing but trees and grass - and, surely, ghosts.

To picture the nave is easier; its outline on the west wall of the abbey is still clear. One arch survives on the south side and two freestanding columns. Two others act as buttresses against the west wall. Rowland Paul's excavations revealed that the nave was 42 metres long and about 9 metres wide. Pace it out and, if you can, imagine it.

But still, without its enormous nave, Dore is glorious. It is a celebration of history. It is also a church which has been in use continuously for 850 years.

Leominster Priory

WHERE CAN YOU FIND A PAIR of affronted birds, affronted snakes, lions and two stooping men? The answer is above the capitals flanking the west door of Leominster Priory.

But the history of this great square church, set apart from the town in its quiet grounds, stretches back to an age long before these figures were carved, which is thought to be about 1130.

In the Dark Ages, around the year 660, Merewald, King of Mercia, who was the son of King Penda, is believed to have founded a monastery at Leominster. Merewald had been converted to Christianity by Edfride, the missionary from Holy Island, and it was Edfride he appointed as the first abbot. How long Merewald's monastery survived no one knows; it is believed to have been destroyed by the Danes.

Some centuries later, during the reign of Edward the Confessor, Leofric, Earl of Mercia, is said to have endowed a nunnery at Leominster. The suggestion allegedly came from his wife, an active supporter of worthy causes. She was Lady Godiva. It may be, as some historians believe, that Leofric simply restored Merewald's earlier monastery. It may also be that his new foundation was not only for nuns but for a mixed community, as was not unusual in Anglo Saxon times. The assumption that it was a nunnery is partly due to a mistranslation of the Welsh name for Leominster, Llanillien. Two 16th century scholars, Leland and Camden, interpreted its meaning as 'the place of nuns'. Later this was revised to 'the church on the streams' - the Rivers Lugg and Kenwater bounded the monastery grounds, the Pinsley Brook is closer still. The most usual explanation for the name is that Leofric's Minster, became Leominster, or Lemster, the spelling still found on some old maps and milestones. In fact it is far more likely that the name simply grew from a corrupted translation of the Welsh.

A further boost to the nunnery theory came from the discovery of 11th century female bones during excavations for a new chancel floor in 1950. Perhaps they were buried there after a plague – or a massacre?

Certainly life for those in Leofric's community, whether male or female, can hardly have been peaceful. Being close to the Welsh border meant that they were frequently under attack and that at some point before the conquest, probably following the capture of the town by Gruffydd ap Llywelyn, Leofric's nunnery was destroyed.

But the threat of violence was not always from the Welsh. In 1046 Sweyn, the eldest son of Earl Godwin and the brother of Harold who later became king, went campaigning in Wales. Things went his way and returning in triumph via Leominster, he burst into the nunnery and captured the Abbess Edgiva, who he 'had as long as he list'. When eventually he'd had enough of the possibly comely and almost certainly ravished Edgiva, he let her go.

In 1121 Henry I, travelling from London to Wales, broke his journey first at Reading, where he laid the foundation stone of a new Abbey, and then at Leominster, where he came upon the ruins of Leofric's nunnery. Following its collapse in the previous century, the site, with its surrounding estates, had reverted to the Crown. Henry decided to establish a monastery there as a cell, or sister house, of his Abbey at Reading. His main motive in founding these communities – there was another sister house at Cholsey in Oxfordshire – was to commemorate his father, William, the Conqueror, his brother, William Rufus, and, most of all, his eldest son, Prince William, who six months before, at the age of seventeen, had been drowned when 'The White Ship', bringing him from Normandy, had been driven onto rocks by the drunken crew. There was one survivor. Among those lost were three of Henry's children. The King, it was said, never smiled again.

Henry's priority therefore was to build churches worthy of those who had died, churches of outstanding magnificence. He appears to have followed the style of the great Benedictine abbey at Cluny in eastern France, where the grandeur of the architecture was reflected in the highly elaborate form of worship.

The abbey at Cluny, founded in 910, became the centre of the Cluniac order which was widely influential throughout Europe. The first Cluniac foundation in England was established soon after the Conquest at Lewes in Sussex.

At Leominster, which like Reading and Cholsey was a Benedictine house, the monks worshipped in the largest and most lavishly decorated Romanesque church in Herefordshire, other than the Cathedral. And their quarters, to the north of the church, were on a similarly grand scale. Yet though they lived in such impressive surroundings, the 'Black Monks' as they were known from the colour of their habits, were forced to live extremely frugally. The reason for this was not simply self denial but because they were close to bankruptcy. This was mainly due to the King.

In founding monasteries at Reading and Leominster, Henry had another less noble motive. The ongoing trouble along the Welsh Border meant that he had to make frequent expeditions to the area. From London the journey took several days; he needed places en route to stop for a meal and a night's rest. Reading, Cholsey and Leominster were ideally situated. Monasteries were renowned for their excellent hospitality. For royal parties which included numerous barons and members of the Household, five star treatment was compulsory. The monasteries found these royal visits, which occurred as frequently during Edward I's reign, a huge financial burden. It was particularly difficult for the daughter houses which had to pay a large percentage of their annual income to Reading Abbey, the mother house. This arrangement lasted right up until the Dissolution. Records show that in 1536 the total revenue from the estates owned by Leominster was £660, from which Reading Abbey was paid £438.

Seven years after Henry had granted the land at Leominster to Reading Abbey, the monastery, built of local sandstone from a quarry at Stretfordbury, was ready for consecration. In 1130 Robert de Bethune, Bishop-elect of Hereford, carried out the ceremony with a consecration cross now kept in a case under the west window of the Priory church.

The church itself was not completed until 1148 when the lay-out consisted of a presbytery, transepts, crossing and a tower, none of which have survived. Of the monastic buildings only the Priory House, as it is now known, still exists. This was added in the 13th century and is thought to have been the infirmary or the reredorter, the lavatories; conveniently underneath the building runs the Pinsley brook. In the late 17th century the Priory House was turned into a gaol, later it became part of a work-house, then an old peoples' home. Now it is unused.

From its earliest time the Priory church of Saint Peter was used not only by the monks but also by the townspeople, who held their services in the western end of the nave. This arrangement was often the cause of trouble between the monks and the parishioners which may have been why, in 1239, another nave was built, replacing the south aisle, for the use of the parish. The new nave was dedicated to Saint Paul.

But disagreement between the monks and the townspeople did not end. At times relations grew so bad that the monks would resort to locking the main doors of the church to keep the parishioners out. When, in 1275, Thomas Cantilupe became Bishop of Hereford, he wrote to the monks urging them emphatically to grant the parishioners their rights. He wrote repeatedly yet apparently without success. In 1284 the Forbury chapel was built a short distance from the Priory which must have eased the situation, even so in 1320 a third nave, or wide south aisle, was added so that there were then three parallel naves each built roughly a century apart.

The Forbury Chapel was given to the Priory by Archbishop Pecham in gratitude for the hospitality provided by the monks while he visited churches and monasteries across the Welsh border. Now in Church Street to the west of the Priory, its dark stone walls stand out among the neighbouring Georgian houses; it is plain slate-roofed, with a triple lancet window in the east wall.

Abruptly in 1539 the life of the monastery came to an end. Henry VIII ordered the dissolution of all large monasteries. (Smaller ones had been dissolved three years earlier.) The monks were dismissed, their monastic buildings and their part of the church was destroyed. Much of the stone disappeared, sold off or stolen; recognisable chunks were discovered later in buildings in the town. But the part of the church used by the townspeople was spared and afterwards, when a new east wall had been built closing off the demolished end, the lay-out of the building was as it is today.

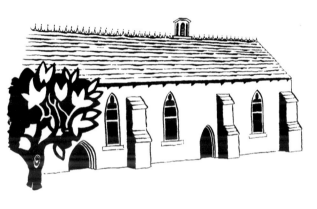

But that was not the end of the forced reforms. During the reign of Edward VI it was ruled that churches must be 'purified', that is purged of all pictures, images and ornaments. All wallpaintings were to be whitewashed and only one chalice and one paten were allowed in each church. At Leominster these are now kept in a wall safe in the south wall of the Priory.

The period following the Dissolution was a bad time for the Priory. Perhaps the presence of the monks with their solemn chanting had been a restraining influence, perhaps without them the feeling was 'anything goes'. For according to the churchwardens' records, there was bad behaviour, lack of reverence. Talking and laughter drowned the preacher's voice and men seldom bothered to remove their

The Black Monks at Leominster divided their time between study and prayer, manual work indoors and out and administering to those in need. Being a cell to Reading the number of monks was probably never very high, though it obviously varied through the years. In 1287, according to Bishop Swinfield's register, the number of monks was under 12.

hats despite the threat of a fine. Dogs, roaming unrestrained, were only kept from the sanctuary by close-set altar rails. The Norman nave was used as a store and a rubbish dump, then it was turned into a burial place.

Perhaps this general lack of respect was part of the climate of the time. Leominster was growing prosperous. This was particularly true during Queen Elizabeth's long reign and was mainly due to the trade in highly prized wool of the Ryeland sheep. More citizens had money to spend on houses, goods, luxuries. Yet, at the same time, arable farming had declined and many farm labourers were redundant. In time they tended to drift into town to look for work, which they seldom found. And since the end of the Wars of the Roses, when many noblemen had disbanded their private armies, countless soldiers had failed to find employment. Despite the Poor Law, vagrants were common; they thronged the streets, begging, thieving, menacing. And the Black Monks were no longer there to give them charity.

Suddenly disaster struck the Priory. Divine retribution some believed. On the 18th of March 1699, while workmen were repairing the roof of the south nave, sparks from their brazier ignited the packing under the lead. Flames flared, spread, burning fiercely. In moments the building was ablaze. Townspeople, crowds of them, rushed to help. Some managed to put out the belfry fire and save the bells. Altar tables were dragged out and a bench or two. Then the whole roof began to burn. Nothing more could be done.

Afterwards a plan was drawn up to rebuild the church on a smaller scale but the townspeople were determined to resist this. A petition signed by 141 citizens was presented to Lord Coningsby of Hampton Court, the Whig M.P. for Leominster, requesting the restoration of their former church. When Lord Coningsby agreed the townspeople set about raising the colossal sum of £16,500, to pay for the rebuilding. The work took six years and, while it was in progress, services were held in the Forbury Chapel. As it measures only 18 by 8 metres the Priory congregation must have been enormously relieved when their spacious church was ready for use again.

Although the size and shape of the church was then as it is today, the Norman nave was still a burial ground filled with earth. Another difference was that the pillars between the central and south naves were round and so out of keeping in a Gothic church. There were also wooden galleries with box stalls underneath in front of the south and west windows. Old photographs show how cluttered the interior appeared.

One wallpainting did survive the Dissolution. It is on the north wall of the nave and dates from about 1275. Though now badly faded it depicts 'The Wheel of Life', a circle enclosing smaller circles and various figures, a design often found on the walls of churches before the Reformation.

In 1861 the new vicar, the Rev. A.G. Edouart, was so shocked at the run down state of the church, that he asked the distinguished architect, Sir George Gilbert Scott, to oversee its restoration. The Norman nave was cleared, the wooden galleries removed, the tower repaired and the round pillars were replaced by a slender Gothic arcade. Altogether the work took nearly 20 years. Since then there have been new stained glass windows; several are by Kempe and one, in the Lady Chapel, is designed by the artist, Martin Travers. Recently the altar has been moved to the middle of the church and where it used to be, at the eastern end, is now the chapel of Saint Paul.

In early medieval times all dogs were required by law to be expeditated, to have the ball of the forefeet cut out to prevent them from hunting the royal deer. King John, visiting Leominster Priory, granted the monks a concession freeing their dogs from being expeditated. This was bitterly resented by the townspeople.

It is a beautiful church, the Priory, full of light and space, with its high painted ceiling in the central nave, its great Norman colonnade along the north aisle. But most remarkable of all, most historically important, are the twelve decorated capitals at the west end. They are outstanding examples of what is known as the Herefordshire School of Romanesque Sculpture. They are indeed so fine that art historians maintain that the name should be changed to the Leominster School. The fact that these particular carvings are all that have survived of the early Romanesque sculpture, gives them added importance. They are special and rare; they link Anglo Saxon art with that of the early Norman age. You need to take time to look at them. You find you do.

All the twelve of these decorated capitals are on attached columns or shafts in the area of the great west door. Possibly the strangest, the most intriguing, is on the left side of the window above the door. It is a design known as the Ring Motif; two rows of rings enclosing doves - each dove is different - are linked through the mouths of sinister masks. Birds appear in two of the other carvings; a bird of prey, a hawk perhaps, attacks a smaller bird, and the affronted doves, stiff-winged with fierce curving beaks. Birds, and in particular doves symbolising the Holy Ghost, were a popular subject of the Herefordshire School. And running like a theme

through almost every carving is what you might call the greenery - or foliage is possibly a better word. There are branches, leaves, trailing stems, some fine, some thick, others gnarled and knotted like ancient vines. In one carving - it is called the 'Palmettes' - the foliage is caught

In the north aisle of the Priory is a ducking stool made in 1718. The last person in England to suffer this humiliating punishment was Jenny Pipes who, in 1809, was tied into this stool and ducked in the Kenwater River.

and bound together then curves apart and is caught again. The affronted serpents coil their long bodies through fan shaped flowers. And the two men, reapers or woodmen, toil in very hoary greenery. They wear what look like striped boiler suits with caps to match and, while their bodies are affronted, their heads are turned so that you see their moustaches, their flat noses and bulging eyes. The lions too turn their heads to stare. They are believed to represent the lion in the legend of Edfride, who turned out to be a gentle beast, sharing bread with the holy man. These lions are watchful, ears pricked, one paw raised. They are not quite sure about Edfride yet.

Inside the west door the foliage is fruitful. Faces, or masks, wreathed in vine leaves spew bunches of grapes through their open mouths. One mask has a plaited double beard, the other, horned, is more beast than man.

There is one more carving, smaller than the rest. Inside the west door, high up on the right hand side, it isn't easy to find. It shows Samson wrestling with the lion. With his long hair flowing down his back, Samson clasps the lion in his arms trying to force its jaws apart. The lion resists, its front paw lifted, its tail curling over its back. So much force, so much action in this tiny carving.

Perhaps in the whole of the Priory it is this that is most remarkable.

Limebrook Priory

OLLOW THE LANE that winds south from Lingen down through the woods to a sheltered valley. And there you are, in Limebrook. There is a mill, a cottage, the brook itself, rushing in winter, meandering when the weather has been dry. There is also a wall, or part of a wall of ivy-smothered stone, standing in a field beside the lane.

If you stop and look over the gate you will see there are parts of the adjoining walls; one, shoulder height, propped against a tree stump, with a gap where there may have been a window, the other, no more than an elongated hump covered in grass. Even so there is enough to show the layout of a cottage, a house, a barn ...

But then beyond these walls, spread out across the field, the acre and a half between the lane and the brook, you notice other mounds, long straight hummocks under the grass suggesting several buildings stood there once, many years ago.

In fact eight centuries ago. The hummocks in the field, the derelict walls, are the ruins of Limebrook Priory, which was founded in 1189 for an order of Augustinian canonesses. These women must have lived there very peacefully in their remote and sheltered valley, drawing water from the brook or possibly a well, said to have existed in the field across the lane.

At that time Limebrook would have belonged to the Mortimer family whose castle at Wigmore was three miles to the north and who, in 1179, had founded the nearby Wigmore Abbey, another Augustinian house. So it seems likely that the Priory at Limebrook was linked to the order at Wigmore Abbey, also to a chapel dedicated to Saint Leonard at a place called the Deerfold a mile to the north. Records show that between 1194 and 1214, Roger Mortimer, the lord of Wigmore, made a grant of land to some 'sisters living in the Deerfold'. Perhaps some of them moved there from Limebrook. We can only guess. There is little trace left of the Deerfold now.

But in recent times research has revealed that these communities, Limebrook, Wigmore and the Deerfold, were far more important than once appeared. They are pieces of an ancient puzzle, clues to the solving of a mystery.

Some years ago it was found that six manuscripts kept in three libraries, the Bodleian in Oxford, Corpus Christi College in Cambridge and the British Library in London, are remarkably alike. All of them are small, five to nine inches high, and have been neatly and clearly written on good quality parchment. These are copies of the original made between about 1225 and 1250; they are clean and have been well preserved. They are addressed to an Augustinian order of anchoresses, religious women who lived in enclosed cells connected to an abbey or church. But, strangely, they are not in Latin as was the custom for written works at that time, nor are they in Norman French which was also sometimes used. They are in English, in a style that is fluent, scholarly, expressive. But, as was the case in the early Middle Ages when both spoken and written English varied according to the region, they have a distinctive dialect. After extensive study historians traced the dialect used in all six manuscripts to the Herefordshire borders.

There was only one place in the area to which they could have belonged; Wigmore Abbey with its sister houses at Limebrook and the Deerfold.

The most important and far the longest work contained in these manuscripts is 'Ancrene Wisse', which roughly means a guide for anchorites or, in this case, anchoresses - 'wisse' is an Anglo-Saxon word. The author speaks directly to 'my dear sisters' urging them, without in any way being heavy and portentous, to live a completely holy life. The prose bounds along, is lively, vivid and readable. The same is true of the other works of instruction; Holy Maidenhead, which praises virginity and does not stint from describing the earthier side of married life, 'the crudities and indecent fooling', and Sawles Warde, which means the soul's keeping and is an allegory introducing such characters as Caution, Strength, Love of Life, who speak of the joys of heaven and the agonies of hell. There are also several prayers and short meditations.

But it is probably the other three works which are the most interesting to lay people. These are 'passions', dramatic presentations of the martyrdom of three heroic female saints, Katherine, Margaret and Juliana. They must be among the earliest of all the medieval mystery plays. The language is vigorous and colourful with a strong rhythm that often sounds like verse, and, although they were partly written for the instruction of the anchoresses alone in their cells, it is clear that two of them at least, 'Margaret' and 'Juliana', – 'Katherine' is more theological – were also intended for public performance. At the start of 'Margaret', for instance, the audience is urged to 'Listen, all you who have ears and hearing, widows along with the wedded ...'.

These passion plays were probably intended to commemorate the feast day of the three saints, to be performed in a hall, a church or market place. Certainly, well acted and directed, they would have provided exciting entertainment. They were something new and apparently popular for we know that, in response to demand, copies were made, according to one source nineteen in a single decade, possibly a record for those times.

And there were copies of Ancrene Wisse, a great many copies, both of the original and a revised version, with scribes from the Franciscan house at Hereford being employed in their production. There is no record of how many were made, but the value of Ancrene Wisse as a handbook and guide must have been widely recognised for it is known to have been in use all over the country right up to the end of the 15th century.

Who wrote it? Scholars puzzled over the question for many years. Then in 1976, after intensive detective work, a book was published by E.J. Dobson that provided the answer.

According to Dobson all six manuscripts were written by one man, a canon belonging to a community near Limebrook, in fact Wigmore. From the high quality of the prose Dobson concludes the canon was a scholar who drew on a large number of sources, and that he was probably from a local family, who may have known the 'dear sisters' personally. Researching records of the region Dobson pinpointed the Lingen family, Norman gentry who had taken the name of a village near Wigmore. He found that early in the 13th century, a younger son, Brian of Lingen, was a secular canon at Wigmore. These facts fit neatly into the puzzle and for the final piece, to provide incontrovertible proof, E.J. Dobson concocts a cryptogram from a phrase buried in one of the manuscripts, combines it with an anagram and up comes a name; Brian of Lingen. It

It was probably in the spring of 1279 that the Bishop of Hereford, Thomas Cantilupe, visited the sisters at Limebrook Priory. He found their discipline lax in several respects; they chattered in the work rooms breaking their rule of silence, they accepted presents breaking their vow of poverty. They were indiscreet in their choice of servants, they also travelled unnecessarily, leaving the Priory for trivial reasons. From his Register we know that Bishop Cantilupe wrote to them - he recommended that the letter be read out several times in either English or French, whichever they knew best - reminding them of their high calling and their solemn vows and advising them to guard the gates of their senses, words he may have borrowed from the Ancrene Wisse.

is Brian of Lingen who wrote the guide, and who acted as confessor to the sisters at Limebrook. Q.E.D. The puzzle is complete.

No one can be sure when Limebrook Priory was abandoned. We know that at the time of the Reformation some of the timber and stone was used to build the nearby cottage. But though so little of the structure has survived, the surroundings cannot be greatly changed; it is still remote, there is still an amazing sense of peace. Perhaps the spirit of Ancrene Wisse hangs in the air ...

Coningsby Hospital

THE CONINGSBY HOSPITAL IS not hard to find. It stands on the east side of Widemarsh Street, one of the roads running north from the middle of Hereford, a long building of reddish sandstone with prominent chimneys and lead-paned windows, odd man out among the shops and offices surrounding it.

Sir Thomas Coningsby founded the Hospital in 1614 for Servitors, who according to Duncomb's History were 'the worn out soldier and the superannuated faithful servant' both, in Coningsby's opinion, sadly neglected by society. He chose the site of an earlier charitable institution, the house of the Knights Hospitaller of the Order of Saint John of Jerusalem, which had been closed down in 1540 during the Dissolution of the Monasteries. The land had been sold to the Coningsby family soon afterwards.

The Herefordshire branch of the Coningsbys, who originally came from Lincolnshire, was by then well established. In 1510 Sir Humphrey, a prominent judge under Henry VIII and great grandfather to Thomas, had bought the estate of Hampton Court near Hope-under-Dinmore.

As a young man Thomas, who was born about 1555, appears adept at making friends in high places. While still in his teens he toured Italy with Sir Philip Sydney. Then in 1591 he set out on a military expedition to Normandy with the Earl of Essex, who appointed him Muster Master of the army. He clearly did well, for that autumn, before the siege of Rouen, he was knighted by the Earl. His diary of the campaign, published by the Camden Society in 1847, gives a first hand picture of military operations at that time. Soon afterwards he was elected as the M.P. for Hereford, for the first time – he achieved it again in 1601. In between he was appointed Sheriff and later to the Council of the Marches and Wales. One of the great and good in fact. Yet he was also known to be slightly odd. His manner and speech were

The Order of St John which began in the 11th century as a hospital for pilgrims to Jerusalem, took on a more military aspect during the crusades. Its members, the Knights Hospitallers, were great rivals of the Templars, a parallel military order founded by French knights during the crusades. After the fall of Acre in 1291 the Hospitallers established themselves in Cyprus, Rhodes, then finally in Malta. Today the headquarters of the Knights of Malta in Rome is the smallest sovereign state in Europe; the current Grand Master, Andrew Barthey, is an Englishman. The Saint John Ambulance Association, founded in Britain in 1877, takes its inspiration from the Order.

generally considered a bit of a joke. Ben Johnson is believed to have modelled an eccentric character in one of his plays on Sir Thomas, 'a vain glorious knight...wholly consecrated to singularity'. Could Sir Thomas have enjoyed his notoriety? But there was criticism too. It was said that he was parsimonious, even downright mean, a reputation that seems unfair for, though he was famously tight-fisted in his dealings with his only surviving son, Fitzwilliam, he did after all build the Hospital, a hugely charitable act.

Why he did so is implied in his introduction to the deed of foundation; he writes of his thankfulness to God for protection during his travels and, enigmatically, 'from malice and evil practices at home'. It seems too that he wished to commemorate the Order of St John with its tradition of providing shelter, originally for pilgrims and crusaders to the Holy Land. In keeping with the Order's military style the head of his new Hospital was known as the Commander and the Servitors wore peaked caps and scarlet coats with the Coningsby crest. When, not long afterwards, Nell Gwyn, whose family home was in Hereford, and who, as the mistress of Charles II, was involved in founding the Chelsea Hospital, she chose a uniform for the Pensioners very similar to that of the Servitors.

Adjoining the south side of Sir Thomas's site were the ruins of the Blackfriars Priory, founded by the Dominicans early in the 14th century when Widemarsh lay outside the medieval city walls. Following the Dissolution there was little left of the Priory but Sir Thomas made use of the loose stone for his Hospital.

He planned it as a quadrangular building; four two-storey blocks surrounding a courtyard, with a stone-tiled roof and trefoil headed windows. Along the south, east and west sides are twelve individual almshouses. The north side contains the chapel and the hall. Here, as part of the medieval structure had survived the Dissolution, it was more a matter of restoration. In the chapel Sir Thomas renewed the three original lancet windows behind the altar and commissioned the artist, Albert van Linge, to design the glass. In a style criticised as being pseudo-Flemish but also praised as rare and remarkable, van Linge's panel pictures The Deposition (the taking down of Christ from the cross). Thomas Coningsby knew William Laud and it seems probable that, like Lord Scudamore, who restored the east window in Dore Abbey, he chose a design that reflected Laud's religious views. Later the van Linge panel was removed and is now in the Victoria and Albert Museum. The present glass in the chapel window shows the Coningsby Arms with three rabbits, or coneys, a rebus on the name, and a Maltese Cross, the badge of the

Knights Hospitallers who later became the Knights of Malta.

On the left facing the door of the chapel are the Coningsby Arms on a stone shield with the letters T.C.P. above, Thomas Coningsby's initials with that of Philippa, his wife.

Adjoining the chapel, the hall with its beamed ceiling is now a museum illustrating the life of the Servitors. There are medals, utensils, spectacles, and photographs of more recent times. Upstairs are lifesize figures; a man sits at a table tucking in to bread and cheese, another, pale and wretched, lies in a truckle bed attended by a nurse, an old man stands proudly in his uniform. As a rule there were eleven Servitors, six retired soldiers or sailors and five servants. All were required to have achieved long service and to have come originally from Hereford or the surrounding area.

Behind the Hospital, on the site of the Blackfriars Priory, is a rose garden. There are also the ruins of a house. This was built by Sir Thomas for himself, partly with the old Priory stone. What remains, the fireplaces, windows and stair turret in the west wall, belong to his time but there are traces still of the original. At the south end of the west wall are three buttresses, further north a possible fireplace as well as what may have been a garderobe. The Dominicans' church, apparently with a spire, was on the south-west side of the monastic buildings. It was consecrated in the presence of Edward III as well as three archbishops. Recent excavations revealed the north wall of the church and part of the adjoining cloister.

On the west side of what is now the rose garden and was once the friars' cemetery, is their preaching cross, the only surviving example of its kind in England. It dates from the 14th century and is hexagonal, standing on four steep steps so that the preaching friar was high above his audience. He could speak in four directions through openwork panels with a stone roof for protection from the rain but without much room to move about. The whole thing looks rather like a mini bandstand with the cross itself high on a pinnacle above the roof.

As you make your way back into the courtyard of the Hospital you notice that behind the almshouses there are gardens, small gardens, carefully tended. They are the gardens of the residents. For still the almshouses are occupied; they are homes, if not for neglected Servitors, for present day Herefordians.

Which would surely please Sir Thomas Coningsby.

Eleanor Gwyn, Nell as she was known, was born in Hereford in 1650. Her family was poor and she first earned her living as an orange girl. Before long, however, being pretty, vivacious and amusing, she succeeded in becoming an actress. She started on the boards at Drury Lane and soon made her name as a comedian, specialising in 'breeches' parts. Her first protector was Lord Buckhurst - and then she met the King. Nell genuinely loved Charles II by whom she had at least one son, Charles Beauclerk, Duke of Saint Albans, born in 1670, and possibly a second, James Beauclerk, born a year later. It is said to have been due to her persuasion that King Charles built Chelsea Hospital.

Nell Gwyn's last stage appearance was in 1682. Five years later, aged only 37, pretty Nellie died.

Bredwardine

IN EARLY SPRING there are violets in the grass, purple and white, outside Saint Andrew's church at Bredwardine. And from nearby fields comes the bleating of lambs. All very pastoral, which is as it should be knowing that the Reverend Francis Kilvert had the living there, knowing his love of the countryside, his gift for describing it day by day.

Kilvert's diaries have become a minor classic. He wrote naturally and lyrically, painting a detailed picture of his life as a Victorian country parson, his parishioners and friends – he had an eye for pretty girls – of celebrations and disasters, illness, blizzards, the Wye in flood.

The Wye is less than quarter of a mile from Bredwardine church which stands above it to the south, next to the vicarage with its large garden, its cedars and terraced lawns.

Kilvert loved Bredwardine. Perhaps not quite as dearly as Clyro, which, a short distance away across the Welsh border, has become known as Kilvert country, but probably because he was the curate at Clyro for seven years, whereas he was only at Bredwardine for two, from 1877 to 1879.

In August 1879 he married Elizabeth Rowland. A month later, suddenly and tragically, he died of peritonitis. He was 39. He was buried at Bredwardine; his granite tombstone is behind a yew tree on the north side of the church. And round the corner, at the western end, is a stone seat in his memory. It is shaded by the branches of another far more ancient yew, its great gnarled trunk leaning drunkenly sideways, towards the north. And inside the church you find this northward tendency echoed in the nave which is angled in the same direction. It makes you wonder if some gargoyle, perhaps the strange monkey-like creature whose head is on the lintel above the north doorway, leapt down one Halloween and gave both the yew and the east end of the church a mighty shove.

The nave is unusually long and narrow. Facing the altar from the west end is rather like looking down a crooked passageway. Herringbone masonry on the north side shows where the original Norman nave was lengthened in the

13th century. A large triple window crowned with graceful tracery gives light to this later part. The chancel was also rebuilt then. But the tower, which is short and square and may have replaced a Norman one, belongs to the late 18th century.

Kilvert tells in his diaries how his father, another country parson, was delighted with the church, its size, its beauty, its tranquillity. He particularly admired the enormous Norman bowl-shaped font, the Norman stonework round the south doorway arch, its lintel decorated with rosettes, as well as the carving over the north door.

It was early January when Kilvert's father visited him at Bredwardine, misty but mild, and although the diary does not tell us so, we can imagine that, emerging from the church, they found the sun shining through the mist, and, as Kilvert writes in another entry, 'the fresh sweet air full of the promise of spring'.

At Bredwardine Francis Kilvert grew his vegetables on the far side of the river Wye. The vicarage kitchen garden was laid out on the site of Brobury House, which was built in the late 19th century.

Bibliography

Alington, Gabriel, *Mappa Mundi* (Gracewing, 1996).

Andere, Mary, *Herefordshire, the Enchanted Land* (Express Logic, 1974).

An Inventory of Historic Monuments in Herefordshire (Volume 1), (South West HMSO, 1931).

Attwater, Donald, *Father Ignatius of Llanthony* (Cassell, 1931).

Cowley, F.G., *The Monastic Order in South Wales 1066-1349* (University of South Wales Press, 1977).

Fancourt, L.D., *Llanthony Priory* (B.A. Hathaway).

Hillaby, Joe, *The Sculptured Capitals of Leominster Priory* (Friends of Leominster Priory Church, 1993).

Hopkins, Gordon, *Llanthony Abbey and Walter Savage Landor* (D. Brown & Sons Ltd, 1979).

Hutchinson, John, *Herefordshire Biographies* (Jakeman & Carver, 4-5 Hightown, Hereford, 1815).

Jancey, E.M., *Saint Ethelbert* (Hereford Cathedral Enterprises, 1994).

Massingham, H.J., *The Southern Marches* (Robert Hale, 1952).

Mason, E.J., *The Wye Valley* (Robert Hale, 1987).

Moorman, R.H., *Church Life in England in the Thirteenth Century* (Cambridge University Press, 1946).

Oman, Charles, *Castles* (Great Western Railway, 1926).

Pevsner, Nikolaus, *Herefordshire* (Penguin Books, 1963), *Shropshire* (Penguin Books, 1958).

Plomer, William (ed.), *Kilvert's Diary 1870-1879* (Jonathan Cape, 1944).

Reeves, N.C., *The Town in the Marches* (Orphans Press, 1972).

Salter, Mike, *Castles of Gwent, Glamorgan and Gower* (Folley Publications, 1991).

Savage, Anne, & Watson, Nicholas (trans.), *Anchoritic Spirituality* (Paulist Press, USA, 1991).

Sledmere, Edwin, *Abbey Dore, its Building and Restoration* (Jakeman & Carver, 1914).

Shoesmith, R., *Castles of Herefordshire* (Logaston Press, 1996).

Shoesmith, R., & Richardson, Ruth, *A Definitive History of Dore Abbey* (Logaston Press, 1997).

Stone, Richard, & Appleton-Fox, Nic, *A View from Herefordshire's Past* (Logaston Press, 1996).

Turton, Eric (comp.), *Leominster* (Chalfont Publishing Co., 1996).